Briefly:
Moore's *Principia Ethica*

The SCM Briefly series

Briefly:
Moore's *Principia Ethica*

David Mills Daniel

scm press

The author and publisher acknowledge material reproduced from
G. E. Moore, *Principia Ethica*, ed. T. Baldwin, Cambridge: Cambridge
University Press, revised edition, 1993, ISBN 0521448484.
Reprinted by permission of the Cambridge University Press.
All rights reserved.

British Library Cataloguing in Publication data

A catalogue record for this book is available
from the British Library

978 0 334 04040 x

First published in 2007 by SCM Press
9–17 St Alban's Place,
London N1 0NX

www.scm-canterburypress.co.uk

SCM Press is a division of
SCM-Canterbury Press Ltd

Typeset by Regent Typesetting, London
Printed and bound in Great Britain by
Bookmarque Ltd, Croydon, Surrey

Contents

Introduction

The SCM *Briefly* series is designed to enable students and general readers to acquire knowledge and understanding of key texts in philosophy, philosophy of religion, theology and ethics. While the series will be especially helpful to those following university and A-level courses in philosophy, ethics and religious studies, it will in fact be of interest to anyone looking for a short guide to the ideas of a particular philosopher or theologian.

Each book in the series takes a piece of work by one philosopher and provides a summary of the original text, which adheres closely to it, and contains direct quotations from it, thus enabling the reader to follow each development in the philosopher's argument(s). Throughout the summary, there are page references to the original philosophical writing, so that the reader has ready access to the primary text. In the Introduction to each book, you will find details of the edition of the philosophical work referred to.

In *Briefly: Moore's Principia Ethica*, we refer to G. E. Moore, *Principia Ethica*, edited by Thomas Baldwin, Cambridge: Cambridge University Press, revised edition, 1993, ISBN 0521448484.

Each *Briefly* begins with an Introduction, followed by a chapter on the Context in which the work was written. Who was this writer? Why was this book written? With Some

Introduction

Issues to Consider, and some Suggestions for Further Reading, this *Briefly* aims to get anyone started in their philosophical investigation. The Detailed Summary of the philosophical work is followed by a concise chapter-by-chapter Overview and an extensive Glossary of terms.

Bold type is used in the Detailed Summary and Overview sections to indicate the first occurrence of words and phrases that appear in the Glossary. The Glossary also contains terms used elsewhere in this *Briefly* guide and other terms that readers may encounter in their study of Moore's *Principia Ethica*.

The text of *Principia Ethica* is divided into 135 sections. Within these, Moore uses numbers and letters (e.g. (1), (a)) to highlight points and issues. The Detailed Summary below is divided into 135 sections, but the numbers and letters are retained only where they fit in with the summarization.

Context

Who was G. E. Moore?

George Edward Moore was born in London in 1873, and educated at Trinity College, Cambridge, where he read classics and moral sciences (philosophy). He was elected a prize fellow of Trinity in 1898, and became a lecturer in philosophy, at the University of Cambridge, in 1911. He was a professor of philosophy there from 1925 to 1939 and editor of the philosophical journal, *Mind*, for over 25 years. Moore was a friend of, and important influence on, the philosophers, Bertrand Russell and Ludwig Wittgenstein (who succeeded him as professor), while his philosophical writings, particularly the emphasis, in *Principia Ethica*, on appreciation of beauty and friendship, were an inspiration to such Bloomsbury Group members as the economist, John Maynard Keynes, the biographer, Lytton Strachey and the novelist, Virginia Woolf.

Along with Russell, Moore rejected absolute idealism (see Glossary), as expressed in the writings of F. H. Bradley and J. M. E. McTaggart (also a fellow of Trinity), which was the dominant philosophical doctrine at the end of the nineteenth century. His emphasis on an analytical approach to philosophical questions, his defence of common sense, particularly in relation to knowledge of the external world, and his interest in metaethics, as a means of clarifying, and trying to resolve, ethical problems, have had a lasting effect on the direction taken by twentieth-century British philosophy. His books include *Principia Ethica* (1903), *Ethics* (1912) and *Some Main Problems of Philosophy* (1953). He died in 1958.

What is *Principia Ethica*?

Principia Ethica, based on a series of lectures on moral philosophy that Moore had delivered a few years earlier, was published in 1903. The title, reminiscent of Newton's *Principia Mathematica*, is indicative of the kind of thorough and systematic study of ethical theory (Moore calls it 'scientific ethics') that the book provides.

As Moore observes, near the beginning of the book, whenever we describe a person or thing as 'good' or 'bad', or say that a particular course of action is 'right' or 'wrong', we are making a moral or ethical judgement. Philosophers have always taken a keen interest in this very common human activity, proposing, investigating and evaluating moral principles and issues, to try to identify what is good and right. However, in the Preface to *Principia Ethica*, Moore makes the point that all this intellectual effort by moral philosophers has not accomplished a great deal, because they have made the mistake of trying to answer ethical questions, without being clear what the questions are. Further, as becomes evident in Chapter I, a lot of moral philosophy has also been characterized by meta-ethical errors: mistakes about the meaning and use of such moral terms as 'good' and 'right'.

So, what are the questions ethics needs to address and answer? According to Moore, there are only two: What sort of things are intrinsically good or good in themselves, that is, have intrinsic value? and What sort of actions ought we to perform, that is, what sort of actions are right? In relation to the first question, Moore holds that ethical propositions about what things are intrinsically good are intuitions: they are directly apprehended, or perceived, and are incapable of proof. Ethical propositions of the second kind, however, are capable of proof, at least in theory. To decide what we ought to do, we first need to know, through intuition, what sort of things are intrinsically good, and then examine the sort of consequences our actions have. This will enable us to choose the course of action that will produce the greatest quantity of things that are intrinsically good.

Thus, as far as goodness is concerned, Moore is an ethical non-naturalist and an intuitionist: he believes that goodness is a non-natural property that a particular thing, or state of affairs, has, which can only be identified by intuition. However, in relation to doing what is right, he is a consequentialist: we need to decide, on the basis of observation and experience, which action will lead to the best possible outcome. He is not a deontological intuitionist: one who holds that what is right can also be known through intuition.

So where have other moral philosophers made their mistakes? Many of them have been wrong about what Moore calls ethics' 'most fundamental question': How is 'good' to be defined? They have been guilty of ethical naturalism, of trying to define or analyse 'good' in terms of a natural property, such as pleasure, or what people desire, holding that 'good' simply means such a natural property. Moore calls defining 'good' as, or confusing it with, a natural property the 'naturalistic fallacy'. Good cannot be defined, because it is a simple, unanalysable, indefinable, non-natural property or quality of things, which is intuited. To say something is 'good' is to say it has this simple, unanalysable quality or property. Complex things (he uses the example of a horse) can be analysed or broken down into their simple or most basic constituent parts, but these will all be objects of thought (Moore gives the example of yellow) that cannot be defined, because they are ultimate terms of reference. Good is one of these.

Even if Moore's definition of 'good' seems rather odd (and agreeing with him about the naturalistic fallacy does not mean having to accept his ethical non-naturalism), this is an extremely important point. Many philosophers, instead of regarding 'good' as indefinable, do define it as a natural property, such as pleasure, or what is desired, and hold that it simply means such a natural property. This clearly is a fallacy because, if good is just defined as a particular property, no other definition can be proved wrong, because what is good is so by definition. Further, unless good and, for example, pleasure are different, saying pleasure is good would be pointless, as it would just be uttering a tautology: pleasure is pleasure. However, stating a tautology is not what people who say pleasure is good believe they are doing: so 'good' cannot just mean pleasure. Moore hammers the point home in another way. However 'good' is defined, it can always be meaningfully asked, of the object in terms of which it is defined, whether it is good. But, if 'good' just means (to stay with the same example) 'pleasure', the question 'Is pleasure good?' would not be intelligible. This is the 'open question' argument: whatever people claim to be good, it is always an open question (one that can be asked meaningfully) whether it is.

Committing the naturalistic fallacy, and failing to appreciate that it is always an open question whether a particular thing is good, are not the only errors moral philosophers have made. Ethical terms, such as 'good', are used in two ways: to say that something is good in itself, or that it is good as means

4

to something that is good in itself. But these two uses are not always distinguished, as they must be, while it is hard to establish that a thing or action definitely is good as a means, because we would need to know (which we hardly ever do) that a certain kind of action would always have a particular effect. Again, many things that are good in themselves are not single things, but complex wholes, and it must not be assumed that the value of a whole is the same as the sum of the values of its parts. Moore gives the example of consciousness of a beautiful object, consisting of the object and consciousness of it. This has great intrinsic value, but a beautiful object seems to have little value, if no one is conscious of it while, if the object is not beautiful, the consciousness is not valuable either. Thus, although a beautiful object and consciousness have great intrinsic value in combination in a whole, when considered separately, they have less or none. Moore gives the name 'organic unity' to what he describes as this 'peculiar relationship' between part and whole. Moral philosophers need to be aware of this principle of organic unities.

Having identified the naturalistic fallacy and other errors in ethical reasoning, Moore goes on to show how frequently they have been committed. He divides ethical theories that commit the naturalistic fallacy into two groups: naturalistic ones, which define 'good' by reference to a natural object, such as pleasure (his not altogether satisfactory test of a natural object is that it exists in time); and metaphysical ones, which define 'good' by reference to what Moore calls 'supersensible reality': thus, someone who defined 'good' in terms of what God commands would be committing a naturalistic fallacy.

Moore divides naturalistic ethical theories into those that maintain that pleasure is the sole good and the (less philosophically important) rest. In Chapter II, he deals with, and dismisses, the latter. Some philosophers argue that there is a natural good, which is fixed by nature. However, it is a fallacy to claim that something is good or bad because it is, or is not, natural. 'Good' does not mean that which is natural, and it is always an open question whether what is natural is good. Moore focuses on the ethical theories of Herbert Spencer, who (Moore argues) seems to misinterpret Darwin's theory of natural selection, thinking that, as human beings are the species fittest to survive in their environment, they are also the 'fittest to fulfil a good purpose'. Spencer commits the naturalistic fallacy of thinking that 'better' means 'more evolved'; but, again, it is an open question whether it is. Moore also accuses Spencer of inconsistency: of being a hedonist, rather than an evolutionist, as he concedes that what is more evolved is only better, if it is also pleasanter.

Moore considers that, as the most commonly committed naturalistic fallacy is in relation to pleasure, which many people think is involved in the definition of good, it is not surprising that hedonism has come to be the most widely held ethical theory. In Chapter III, he considers hedonistic theories, and accuses the major nineteenth-century British philosopher, John Stuart Mill of committing the naturalistic fallacy in his book *Utilitarianism*. In it, Mill maintains that pleasure or happiness is desirable (in Moore's terms, 'good as an end'), and the only thing desirable as an end, while other things are only desirable as means to it. The proof Mill offers is an analogy with visibility. Their being seen is the only proof that things are visible, so the only proof that something is desirable is that people desire it. People desire happiness individually, while general happiness is the happiness of the aggregate of all persons. Moore labels Mill's argument a 'naïve' use of the naturalistic fallacy, because Mill has not given 'desirable' its proper meaning. 'Desirable' does not mean 'able to be desired', but 'what ought to be desired'.

Moore points out what he sees as further flaws in Mill's argument. As he has (wrongly) defined 'good' as 'desired', to show that pleasure alone is good, he must now prove that it is the only thing people desire as an end. However, people clearly desire other things as ends, such as money or virtue. Mill argues that there is no real conflict here. Other things are desired (initially) as a means to happiness, but become so closely identified with it that they come to be regarded as part of it. Moore is not convinced: Mill has been forced to eliminate the distinction between means and ends, due to his failure to distinguish 'end', in the sense of what is desirable, from 'end', in the sense of what is desired. Moore also challenges the basis of Mill's psychological hedonism. He accepts that there is a link between pleasure/happiness and desire, but it does not support hedonism. While Mill holds that the idea of a pleasure, not actual, is always necessary to cause desire, in fact it is caused by an actual pleasure, produced by the idea of having something else. He gives the example of a glass of port: the idea of drinking the port produces a feeling of pleasure in the mind, which leads to a desire for the port. Mill's psychological hedonism confuses a pleasant thought with the thought of a pleasure: when there is only a pleasant thought, it is the object of the thought that is the object of desire.

Is Moore's criticism of Mill fair? While Mill seems to commit the naturalistic fallacy, it has been argued, in his defence, that he does not claim to be offering a strict proof that happiness is desirable as an end, but rather inviting his readers to observe what their fellow human beings actually value. Again, Mill concedes that questions of ultimate ends are not capable of direct proof. His own view is that pleasure is the only thing that people desire as an end, but he asks people to look around them, and test his opinion by observing themselves and others. Moore acknowledges that Mill is not attempting a strict demonstration of his theory, but perhaps he criticizes him as if he were offering one, rather than what Mill calls an 'indirect proof'.

Moore accepts that the hedonistic principle, that only pleasure is good as an end, may be true, but this can be known only by intuition. However, there are considerations that incline the mind against it. One of these is Mill's own argument, again in *Utilitarianism*, that pleasures differ in quality. Moore argues that this is inconsistent with hedonism because, if pleasures differ qualitatively, they must be complex, consisting of pleasure and what produces it. Introducing different qualities of pleasure rules out the claim that pleasure alone is good as an end: there must be something in the higher-quality pleasures, not present in all pleasures, and which is also good as an end; but this is incompatible with the hedonistic principle.

Moore also discusses Henry Sidgwick's intuitionistic hedonism, as set out in his *The Methods of Ethics*. Against Sidgwick, Moore asks if pleasure is valuable in itself, or only when human beings are conscious of it, as a person could lead a life of intense pleasure, while lacking intelligence, memory or knowledge. In fact, pleasure does not seem valuable without consciousness of it, suggesting that pleasure cannot be the only desirable thing, as consciousness of it is more desirable still. Sidgwick may consider that regarding happiness as only part of what is ultimately good does not fit in with the facts of intuition, but he ignores the principle of organic unities. The fact that enjoyment of beauty is valuable, while just contemplating it is not, does not mean that all the value lies in the pleasure. It does not follow that, because there is no value in one part of an organic whole, by itself, all the value is in the other part: both may be equally necessary parts of something intrinsically good, but (comparatively) valueless by themselves. Sidgwick fails to ask whether pleasure, by itself, would have much value. As pleasure seems a necessary element in most valuable wholes, it is easy to think that, if the other elements lack value by themselves, all the value lies in it. In reality, when judging thing as ends, people often prefer less pleasant to more pleasant states, agreeing with Mill that there are higher and more valuable pleasures.

Moore also dismisses egoism, which holds that each individual should pursue his own happiness as his ultimate end: if each person's happiness is the sole good, more than one thing is the sole good, which is contradictory.

In Chapter IV Moore turns to ethical theories which hold that ethical truths follow from metaphysical ones. But this also commits the naturalistic fallacy, because 'good' can no more be defined in terms of a supersensible property than in terms of a natural one. Even if the existence of a supersensible reality could be established, it would still be an open question whether it is good. The nature of a supersensible reality could be relevant to what we ought to do, if it could show we are immortal and how our present conduct affects our future condition. He also thinks that Kant is wrong to discuss (obedience to) the moral law in terms of (categorical) imperatives, as this equates what ought to be with what is commanded, when what is commanded is only a source of moral obligation, if it is good; and rejects (as they commit the naturalistic fallacy) arguments that suggest that what is good is what is willed, or willed in a particular way.

Chapter V addresses the question of what is right, or what we ought to do, which involves both ethical judgements about what is good in itself and empirical investigation of the kind of effects particular actions produce. When ethics prescribes duties, it means acting in ways that will always produce the greatest possible sum of good. This is where Moore's intuitionism differs from that of the deontological intuitionists, who maintain that what is right is, like what is good in itself, intuitively certain. However, Moore does not believe that ethics can give a definite list of duties. This would require information about all the future effects of a possible action and their value, but even establishing the probability that a particular action will produce a better total result than another is very difficult. All practical ethics can do is lay down general rules about which of a few alternative actions will generally produce the greatest balance of good in the short term. Given how hard it is to calculate the consequences of actions, people should generally abide by the rules of common-sense morality, such as those prohibiting murder, as experience has shown they are essential to the preservation of civilized society. Indeed, a generally practised rule should always be followed for, even though it may not always be appropriate, people are unlikely to be able to decide correctly when it will not be, and they will set a bad example to others, if they do not follow it. Thus, Moore advocates an extremely conservative attitude towards well-established, common-sense rules of morality: only when there is no generally practised rule to hand, should people consider the intrinsic value or badness of the effects of possible actions, and act accordingly. Virtues, which Moore defines as a 'habitual disposition' to carry out actions that usually 'produce the best possible results', are generally regarded as having intrinsic value, but the same test of whether they are a means to good should be applied to them as to duties.

What does Moore consider to have the highest value: what

is his ideal? In Chapter VI, he contends that one problem with many accounts of the ideal has been omitting many things of positive value, by limiting them to the best of single things. But there are many positive goods, and any whole containing them must be a complex one. Determining the ideal involves identifying things that would be judged good, if they existed by themselves, and then determining their comparative value. Moore has no doubt that the most valuable things are the pleasures of human relationships and enjoyment of beautiful objects. Moral philosophy's fundamental truth is that it is only for their sake that there is any purpose in doing any public or private duty, or being virtuous. He considers that these complex wholes are the rational ultimate end of human action. This chapter also contains discussion of great positive evils. There are three types: admiring contemplation, or love, of what is evil, as in cruelty and lust; mixed evils, which involve cognition of what is good, together with an inappropriate emotion, as in hating the good; and pain, which would not be an evil without consciousness of it. Moore defines mixed goods as positively good wholes, which contain intrinsically evil elements, as with such virtues as courage and compassion, which require cognition of something evil and hatred of it. One interesting point Moore makes is that, although the appropriate mental attitude towards a real evil is a positive good, the really existing evil always brings the total sum of value down to a negative amount. Therefore, the argument in some (Christian) theodicies, that actual suffering must exist, so that compassion can be felt for it, has to be rejected. There is no justification for the existence of even the least of the world's actual suffering: imaginary suffering would be sufficient for the development of compassion.

Principia Ethica has been criticized on a number of

grounds. Given the range of possibilities, Moore's view that the pleasures of human relationships, and enjoyment of beautiful objects, are the rational ultimate end of human action may seem eccentric. His ethical non-naturalism and intuitionism seem to make identification of what is good a highly individual and mysterious process, and to turn moral debate into an exchange of different intuitions. His caution about our ability to calculate the consequences of our actions appears excessive, while his insistence that people should always abide by generally practised rules of morality would prevent departures from them, even when the circumstances clearly warrant doing so, and would make it hard to challenge accepted moral principles, even if they are in need of reform. Moore's harsh criticisms of Mill, and his judgement that the latter made a naïve use of the naturalistic fallacy, do not appear to do justice to the arguments Mill puts forward in *Utilitarianism*. However, *Principia Ethica* is a landmark in British philosophy. Its emphasis on metaethics, its concern with the nature of moral argument and the meaning and use of moral terms and, in particular, Moore's identification of the naturalistic fallacy and the open-question argument, made an invaluable contribution to moral philosophy, and played a major a part in determining the direction it would take in the twentieth century.

Some Issues to Consider

- Moore argues that moral philosophers have gone wrong, because they have tried to answer ethical questions, without being clear what the questions are, and have made mistakes about the meaning and use of such moral terms as 'good' and 'right'.

- There are only two ethical questions to answer: What sort of things are good in themselves? and What sort of actions ought we to perform?
- Moore holds that ethical propositions about what things are intrinsically good are intuitions: they are directly apprehended or perceived, and are incapable of proof.
- According to Moore, when we are deciding what we ought to do, we first need to know what sort of things are intrinsically good, and then choose the course of action that will produce the greatest quantity of things that are intrinsically good.
- Good is a simple, unanalysable, indefinable, non-natural property or quality of things.
- Moore calls defining 'good' as a natural property the 'naturalistic fallacy'.
- Whatever is claimed to be good, it is always an open question whether it is.
- Many things that are good in themselves are not single things, but complex wholes, and it must not be assumed that the value of the whole is the same as the sum of the values of its parts.
- It is a naturalistic fallacy to define 'good' as a natural property or what is more evolved.
- Does John Stuart Mill make a naïve use of the naturalistic fallacy in *Utilitarianism*?
- Moore holds that a desire is caused by an actual pleasure, produced by the idea of having something else: for example, the idea of drinking port produces a feeling of pleasure, leading to a desire for the port.
- Is Mill's view that there are different qualities of pleasure inconsistent with hedonism?
- According to Moore, it does not follow that, because there

is no value in one part of an organic whole, by itself, all the value lies in the other part.

- As pleasure seems a necessary element in most valuable wholes, it is easy to think that, if the other elements lack value by themselves, all the value lies in it.
- It is just as much of a naturalistic fallacy to define 'good' in terms of a supersensible reality as a natural one.
- Ethics cannot give a definite list of duties, because we cannot know all the future effects of a possible action and their value.
- As it is hard to calculate the consequences of actions, people should generally abide by the rules of common-sense morality, such as those prohibiting murder, as experience has shown they are essential to the preservation of civilized society.
- Moore believes that the most valuable things are the pleasures of human relationships and enjoyment of beautiful objects. Do you agree with him?
- There are three types of great positive evils: love of what is evil; mixed evils, which involve cognition of what is good, together with an inappropriate emotion; and pain.

Suggestions for Further Reading

G. E. Moore, *The Elements of Ethics*, ed. T. Regan, Philadelphia: Temple University Press, 1991.

G. E. Moore, *Ethics*, ed. W. H. Shaw, Oxford: Clarendon Press, 2005.

G. E. Moore, *Philosophical Papers*, London: Allen and Unwin, 1959.

G. E. Moore, *Philosophical Studies*, London: Routledge, 2000.

Suggestions for Further Reading

G. E. Moore, *Principia Ethica*, ed. T. Baldwin, revised edition, Cambridge: Cambridge University Press, 1993.

G. E. Moore, *Selected Writings*, ed. T. Baldwin, London: Routledge, 1993.

G. E. Moore, *Some Main Problems of Philosophy*, London: Routledge, 2002.

A. J. Ayer, *Russell and Moore: The Analytical Heritage*, London: Macmillan, 1973.

W. D. Hudson, *Modern Moral Philosophy*, London: Palgrave Macmillan, 1983.

B. Hutchinson, *G. E. Moore's Ethical Theory: Resistance and Reconciliation*, Cambridge: Cambridge University Press, 2001.

I. Kant, *Groundwork of the Metaphysics of Morals*, ed. M. Gregor, Cambridge: Cambridge University Press, 1998.

J. S. Mill, *Utilitarianism*, ed. G. Sher, second edition, Indianapolis/Cambridge: Hackett Publishing Company, 2001.

P. A. Schlipp, *The Philosophy of G. E. Moore*, La Salle: Open Court Publishing, 1977.

H. Sidgwick, *The Methods of Ethics*, seventh edition, Indianapolis: Hackett, 1991.

G. J. Warnock, English Philosophy since 1900, Oxford: Oxford University Press, 1969.

Detailed Summary of G. E. Moore's
Principia Ethica

Preface to The First Edition (pp. 33–7)

One of the main problems with **ethics** is trying to 'answer questions' without clearly identifying the question; but doing so might eliminate many of **philosophy**'s biggest 'difficulties and disagreements' (p. 33). In this book, I have attempted to distinguish 'two kinds of question' that '**moral philosophers**' have 'professed to answer': what sort of things should '**exist for their own sakes**' (things with '**intrinsic value**'), and what sort of actions 'ought we to perform' (**right actions** or **duties**) (pp. 33–4)? A further issue concerns the sort of evidence that can prove or disprove an 'ethical **proposition**' (p. 34). But, once we understand the questions, it is clear that there is 'no relevant evidence' in relation to ethical propositions of the first kind; error can only be avoided by ensuring that we are addressing that question and not a different one (p. 34). The second is capable of 'proof or disproof', but many different, relevant considerations make even 'attainment of **probability**' very difficult (p. 34). However, the '*kind* of evidence' can be defined exactly: it consists of both 'truths with regard to the results' ('*causal* **truths**') and '**ethical truths of our first or self-evident class**' (p. 34). So, if a moral philosopher gives 'any evidence whatever' for the first kind of ethical proposition, or fails to provide 'both causal and ethical truths' for the second, he is unlikely to be able 'to establish his conclusions' (pp. 34–5).

A 'main object' of this book is to identify the '**fundamental principles of ethical reasoning**' (p. 35). However, Chapter VI suggests some answers to the question, '"What is good in itself?"' that are 'different' from those of most moral philosophers (p. 35). I maintain that many things are '**good and evil in themselves**', and that these possess no '**common**' or '**peculiar**' **properties** (p. 35).

To make it plain that the first kind of ethical propositions cannot be proved or disproved, I have called them '"**Intuitions**"' (p. 35). But, I am not an 'Intuitionist' in the usual sense of holding that ethical propositions of my second kind (that assert the rightness of particular actions) cannot be proved or disproved by examining their results (p. 35). Calling the first kind of ethical propositions 'Intuitions' is just a way of saying they are 'incapable of proof'; it has nothing to do with 'our **cognition** of them' (p. 36). Unlike most intuitionists, I am not saying a proposition is true because of how we 'cognise' it (p. 36). Before finishing the book I found, in one by **Brentano**, views very like mine. However, he thinks the 'fundamental ethical concept' is not the 'simple one' that 'I denote by "good"', but the 'complex one' I have taken 'to define "beautiful"'; and he appears to deny what I have termed '*the **principle of organic unities**'* (p. 36). Thus, while he agrees there are 'many different goods', and that 'the love of good and beautiful objects' is an important class of them, we differ 'very materially' about 'what things are good in themselves' (p. 36).

One of this book's weaknesses is that it does not directly discuss the different ideas 'expressed by the word "**end**"' (p. 37).

Rewriting the book might produce a different and better one, but also make the ideas I am most keen to get across 'more obscure' so, though aware of its 'defects', it is probably best to publish it 'as it stands' (p. 37).

Trinity College, Cambridge, August, 1903

The book is being reprinted, as I still agree with its main 'conclusions' (p. 37). I have not altered it, because to start doing so would lead to rewriting the whole of it.

Cambridge, 1922

Chapter I (pp. 53–88)

The Subject Matter of Ethics

1 The truth of some of our 'every-day judgments' certainly involves ethics, as when we call someone a 'good man', or ask, 'What ought I to do?' (p. 53). When we make statements containing such terms as 'duty, right, ought, good, bad, we are making ethical judgments', but this does not define the 'province of Ethics' (p. 53). We need to ask what is 'common and peculiar' to these 'judgments'; and different moral philosophers have given 'very different answers' to this question (p. 53).

2 All these judgements concern 'conduct' (p. 53). When we say someone 'is good', we mean 'he acts rightly', or when we condemn drunkenness, we indicate it is a 'wicked action' (p. 54). Some **'ethical philosophers'** think that ethics is just 'what is good or bad in human conduct', but 'good conduct' is a 'complex **notion**', and there are other things, besides conduct, which are good; so, 'good' refers to some common 'property' they and conduct have (p. 54). Limiting ethics to

19

conduct may mean not knowing even what 'good conduct' is (p. 54). I shall consider 'what is good in general', and 'what is bad' (pp. 54–5).

3   But we must take care. Lots of statements can give some sort of answer to the question, 'What is good?', but not in the sense that '**scientific Ethics**' does (p. 55). Many answers to this question can form no 'part of an ethical system', but belong to such 'studies' as 'history, geography, astronomy' (p. 55).

4   The question, 'What is good?' may be given 'another meaning': 'Pleasure is good' would be an answer to it (p. 55). And this, though less important than the judgement '**Pleasure** *alone* **is good**', is one ethics should discuss (pp. 55–6). Judgements of the same sort are dealt with in '**Casuistry**', seen as 'much less respectable' than ethics, but differing from it 'only in degree', as it is more 'particular', concerning 'what actions are good, *whenever they occur*' (p. 56). Casuistry is not satisfied with 'the **general law** that **charity** is a **virtue**', but tries to discover the 'relative merits' of its different forms (p. 56). But it is 'too difficult a subject to be treated adequately in our present state of knowledge' (p. 57).

5   There is a third possible meaning: 'how "good" is to be defined', and this is ethics' 'most fundamental question' (p. 57). Indeed, unless this question is 'fully understood' and 'its true answer' given, the 'rest of Ethics is as good as useless', as no one will 'know *what is the evidence* for any ethical judgment' (p. 57).

6   'How is good to be defined' (p. 58)? This is not a **lexicographical question** about 'proper usage' of the term, but concerns the 'object or idea' the word is 'generally used to stand for' (p. 58). My answer may seem 'disappointing': 'good is good', and 'cannot be defined' (p. 58). But, this is an important point; it means that 'propositions about the good are all of

them **synthetic** and never **analytic**', so nobody can force upon us such **axioms** as, 'Pleasure is the only good', or, 'The good is the desired', on the basis that this is the word's 'very meaning' (pp. 58–9).

7 'Good' is a 'simple notion', like yellow, and cannot be defined. It is not like a horse, which can be defined (p. 59), because it has 'many different **properties**': although, once a horse has been reduced to 'his **simplest terms**', these cannot be defined (p. 59). They are 'simply something which you think of or perceive', the nature of which cannot be 'known' to those unable to do so (p. 59). The objection that we can describe to others objects they have 'never seen or thought' does not stand, because they will be 'complex' objects, 'reducible to simplest parts' (p. 59). However, 'yellow and good' are 'notions of that simple kind', from which 'definitions are composed and with which the power of further defining ceases' (pp. 59–60).

8 When I 'deny good to be definable', I mean that, unlike a horse, it does not consist of 'parts', such as 'legs, a head, a heart' (p. 60). We might think of a horse as 'its parts', not 'the whole', but there is nothing we could 'substitute for good' (p. 60).

9 This is not to say that '*the* good' is indefinable, so I should explain 'the difference' between 'the good' and '*good*' (p. 60). '"Good" is an adjective', while 'the good' is 'the **substantive**', to which it applies: which means it is 'different from that adjective itself', and other adjectives, such as 'pleasure' and 'intelligence', may 'apply to it' (p. 61). I accept that 'some true proposition of the form, "Intelligence is good and intelligence alone is good", can be found' (p. 61). If this were not the case, 'definition of *the* good would be impossible'; but 'good itself is indefinable' (p. 61).

10 So, '"good" has no definition because it is simple and

21

has no parts'; it is one of many 'objects of thought' that cannot be defined, because they are 'ultimate terms' of reference (p. 61). There are bound to be an 'indefinite number' of them (p. 61). We define things 'by an **analysis**' that ultimately 'refers us to something which is simply different from anything else' (pp. 61–2). Yellow is another example of a 'simple and indefinable' quality (p. 62). Now, just as yellow things 'produce a certain kind of vibration in the light', it may be that all good things 'are *also* something else'; and the aim of ethics is to discover 'those other properties' (p. 62). But many **philosophers** have believed that, by listing them, they have defined 'good', because they are 'the same' as goodness (p. 62). I call this the '**naturalistic fallacy**' (p. 62).

11   These philosophers do not agree among themselves; one argues that 'good is pleasure', another 'that which is desired' (p. 62). Let us take the attempted proof of the latter claim. (1) It may be an attempt to 'prove that the object of desire is not pleasure': in which case, where is the 'Ethics' (p. 63)? Even proving 'a million times over' that 'pleasure is not the object of desire' would not prove 'his opponent' wrong (p. 63). It is like one person saying 'a triangle is a circle', another that it is 'a straight line' (p. 63). All that can be proved is that one of them is wrong, because 'a triangle cannot be both a straight line and a circle' (p. 63). If good is just *'defined* as something else', there is no possibility of proving 'any other definition' wrong (p. 63). (2) It may be a merely '**verbal**' **discussion**, with the propositions that 'good' means 'pleasant' or 'desired' being about people's use of the word (p. 63). This may result in an 'interesting' discussion, but not an 'ethical' one (p. 63). We wish to learn, not 'how people use a word', but 'what *is* good' (p. 64).

12   If someone says he is pleased, he means he has a 'definite

feeling called pleasure', which is one 'absolutely indefinable' thing (p. 64). We can 'describe its relations to other things', for example, that 'it causes desire', but not 'define' it (p. 64). If someone attempts to define pleasure as another '**natural object**', such as 'the sensation of red', we 'laugh at him'; but his suggestion would be 'the same **fallacy** which I have called the naturalistic fallacy' (pp. 64–5). That pleasure is 'absolutely indefinable' does not make it difficult to know and say when we are pleased (p. 65). Further, there is no difficulty in saying, 'pleasure is good'; but this does not mean that 'pleasure *means* good', or vice versa (p. 65). If two 'natural objects' are confused, there is 'no reason to call the fallacy naturalistic', but when 'good', which is not 'in the same sense a natural object', is confused with a natural object, there is: it is 'quite specific', and merits a name, as 'it is so common', being found 'in almost every book on Ethics' (p. 65). Let us think of the confusion there would be, if we insisted that, because 'an orange is yellow' it, and every other yellow object, '*meant* exactly the same thing as yellow' (p. 66). We would have to accept that an orange was 'the same' as, say, 'a lemon': leading to our being able to prove all sorts of 'absurdities' (p. 66). It is the same with good. It does not follow from the fact that 'good' is 'indefinable' that I have 'to deny that pleasure is good' (p. 66). Indeed, 'unless good is something different from pleasure', there is 'no meaning in saying that pleasure is good' (p. 66).

13   If 'good' does not denote 'something simple and indefinable', the only serious 'alternatives' are that it is a 'complex' whole, about 'correct analysis' of which there is 'disagreement', or that 'it means nothing at all' (p. 66). However, when 'ethical philosophers have attempted to define good', they have not 'seriously' considered 'these possibilities' (pp. 66–7). **(1)** The '**hypothesis** that disagreement about the meaning of good' is one about 'correct analysis' of a whole is clearly wrong, because, '**whatever definition' of 'good' is given, it 'may always be asked, with significance, of the complex so defined, whether it is itself good**' (p. 67). Let us take one common definition of 'good': that it is 'that which we desire to desire' (p. 67). It seems 'plausible', but the question, 'Is it good to desire to desire A?' is just as 'intelligible' as the question, 'Is A good?' (p. 67). We cannot 'correctly' analyse the second question's meaning into: 'Is the desire to desire A one of the things which we desire to desire?' (p. 67). Clearly, 'the **predicate** of this proposition – "good" – is positively different from the notion of "desiring to desire" which enters into its subject' (p. 67). Even if what we 'desire to desire is always also good', the fact that we can understand 'what is meant by doubting it' proves we have 'two different notions before our minds' (pp. 67–8). **(2)** As for the second alternative, it is 'easy to conclude that what seems to be a **universal ethical principle** is in fact an **identical proposition**': specifically, that because 'whatever is called "good" seems to be pleasant', the 'proposition, "Pleasure is the good", does not assert a connection between two different notions', but is about 'only one': pleasure (p. 68). But, when we enquire whether pleasure is good, we are not asking, 'whether pleasure is itself pleasant' (p. 68). And this applies to every 'suggested definition' of 'good' (p. 68). Whenever someone thinks about what has '**intrinsic worth**', or whether something 'ought to exist', he 'has before his mind the unique object ... which I mean by "good"' (p. 68). And, for 'correct ethical reasoning', it is vital to recognize 'this fact' (pp. 68–9).

14   Only **Sidgwick** has recognized that 'good' is an 'indefinable' or 'unanalysable notion', and he gives an example that shows the vital importance of 'this principle' (p. 69). **Bentham** states that 'the **greatest happiness** of all those whose interest

is in question' is the 'right' end of 'human action' (p. 69). Elsewhere, though, he appears to say that 'conducive to the **general happiness**' is what 'right' means (p. 69). This seems so 'absurd' that Sidgwick suggests 'Bentham cannot have meant it' (p. 69).

Certainly, Bentham's '**fundamental**' **moral principle** seems to involve a 'naturalistic fallacy', which **Mill** also committed (p. 69). Bentham might have used 'right' to denote what is '**good as a means**', leaving open the question of whether it is 'also good as an end'; and this is how I shall always use the word (p. 70). If he was using 'right' in this way he might, quite consistently, have defined it as 'conducive to the general happiness', as long as he had proved, or stated, that 'general happiness was *the* good' (p. 70). Then, as 'right' was to be 'defined as "conducive to *the* good"', it would '*mean* "conducive to general happiness"' (p. 70). But Bentham applies the word 'right' to 'the end, as such', not just to the means of attaining it, and so commits the naturalistic fallacy (p. 70). If 'right' is defined as 'conducive to general happiness', obviously, 'general happiness is the right end' (p. 70). Thus, the statement that 'general happiness' is 'the right end' of human action becomes, not 'an **ethical principle**' about its 'rightness or goodness', but a statement about the 'meaning of words', or 'the *nature* of general happiness' (p. 71).

This is not to say that Bentham's claim that 'greatest happiness is the proper end of human action' is wrong; but, to the extent that it involves 'a definition of right', the '*reasons*' he gives for his 'ethical proposition' are (p. 71). Had Bentham realized this, he would have looked for 'other reasons' to support 'his **Utilitarianism**', might have found none, and changed 'his whole system'; or identified ones he thought adequate: but use of the naturalistic fallacy gravely weakens his position

(p. 71). Ethics' 'direct object' is 'knowledge and not practice'; any 'true results' must be based on **'valid reasons'** (p. 71). One who uses the naturalistic fallacy will not achieve this object, 'however correct his **practical principles**' (p. 71). '**Naturalism**' gives no 'valid reason' for an 'ethical principle', and leads to 'acceptance' of false ones (pp. 71–2). If we start with the view that 'good' means one particular 'property of things', we shall limit ethical enquiry to discovering it (p. 72). But, if we accept that 'anything whatever may be good', we shall begin with a 'more open mind' (p. 72). Further, if we 'think we have a definition' of 'good', we shall be unable to 'defend our ethical principles' **logically**, and will probably 'misunderstand our opponent's arguments', or try to silence them with the assertion that the matter is 'not an **open question**: the very meaning of the word decides it' (p. 72).

15   Our 'first conclusion' was that there is a 'simple', 'unanalysable object of thought' that defines the 'subject-matter of Ethics', and that the words 'commonly taken as the signs of ethical judgements all do refer to it' (p. 72). But there are two ways in which they 'refer to that unique notion which I have called "good"': they may state that it attaches 'to the thing in question' (that the thing is 'good in itself'), or that the thing is 'a cause or *necessary* **condition**' of 'other things' to which 'this unique property' attaches (that the thing is 'good as means') (p. 73). Many 'difficulties' in 'ordinary' ethical discussion arise from not distinguishing between these 'two species of **universal ethical judgments**'. The 'distinction' is 'as follows' (p. 73).

16   Judging something 'good as a means' is saying it has 'a particular kind of effect' that is 'good in itself' (p. 73). However, **universally true 'causal judgments'** are hard to find and, for correct ethical judgements, we would need to know **(1)**: that

a certain kind of action would produce such an 'effect' in all '*circumstances*' (pp. 73–4). But this is 'impossible'; the best we can hope for is a 'generalisation' that such an effect '*generally* follows this kind of action' (p. 74). So, no 'ethical' judgement that a 'certain kind of action is good as a means to a certain kind of effect' is going to be '*universally* true' (p. 74). We would need to know **(2)**: that the action would not only produce '*one* good effect', but that, in its effect on 'all subsequent events', the '**balance of good**' would be 'greater' than from any possible alternative (p. 74).

Saying an action is 'generally a means to good' is saying, not only that it 'generally does *some* good', but that it 'generally does the greatest good' that 'the circumstances admit' (p. 74). But, we can never know this, and must be content with what seems to be 'the greatest possible balance of good' over a limited period (p. 74). This is of great 'practical importance' in ethical debate, and we must remember that our '**commonest rules of conduct**' do allow for balancing future losses against 'immediate gains' (p. 75). We can never be sure of achieving 'the greatest possible total of good', but must try to prevent any 'probable future evils' of our actions exceeding 'the immediate good' they produce (p. 75).

17 Judgements, stating that 'certain kinds of things have good effects', are **(1)** 'unlikely to be true', if they claim they '*always*' do, and **(2)**, even if they just state that they '*generally*' do, this will only apply at certain times in history; but judgements, stating that 'things are themselves good' will, 'if true at all', be 'universally true' (p. 75). We must distinguish these 'two kinds' of judgements, as ethics is about 'a limited class of actions', of which we may ask, 'how far they are good in themselves' and, how far their 'general tendency' is to 'produce good results' (pp. 75–6). 'Ethical philosophers' have not

27

noticed these are 'the only questions' ethics has to settle, or that settling one is '*not* the same' as settling the other: which may be due to the '**ambiguous form**' of ethical questions (p. 76). A question like, 'Is it right to act in this way?', covers both 'what is good in itself and causal judgments' (p. 76). If an action is '*the* best thing to do', it will produce 'a **greater sum of intrinsic value**' than possible alternatives; an 'absolutely right or **obligatory** action' will cause 'more good or less evil' to 'exist in the world' than 'any possible alternative'; and saying an action will have particular 'consequences' is to make 'a number of causal judgments' (pp. 76–7). When we ask what we ought to aim at securing, we can easily overlook the 'obvious' point that we must specify 'something which *can* be secured', as not everything can (p. 77). So, neither judgements about what we ought to do, nor those about 'the ends' our actions 'ought to produce', are 'pure judgements of intrinsic value' (p. 77). An action, though devoid of 'intrinsic value', may be 'absolutely obligatory' by causing 'the best possible effects' (p. 77). These 'justify our action', but have 'intrinsic value' only to the extent that 'the **laws of nature**' permit (p. 77). So, when trying to decide what we ought to do, we need to know, not only the 'degree of intrinsic value different things have', but also how they 'may be obtained' (p. 77). All 'practical' ethical questions involve 'this double knowledge', but are invariably debated without the two being distinguished, resulting in the views that either 'nothing has intrinsic value which is not possible', or 'that what is necessary must have intrinsic value' (pp. 77–8). It has also led to neglect of both the central concern of ethics, which is deciding what things have 'intrinsic value', and of '*thorough* discussion of means', as this is judged 'irrelevant to the question of intrinsic values' (p. 78). But 'what is best in itself', and what will achieve the 'best possible' results, are both 'distinct' questions, which are part of ethics (p. 78).

18 A further point is that there are 'different things' that have 'intrinsic value', 'positively bad' things, and apparently '**indifferent**' things, any one of which may be 'part of a whole' that comprises things from 'the same' and 'the other two classes', while 'the wholes' may also 'have intrinsic value' (p. 79). Two good things may make a whole of 'immensely greater' value than the 'sum of the values' of these two good things; two bad things may make a whole 'much worse than the sum of badness of its parts'; and so on (p. 79). The important point here is: '*The value of a whole must not be assumed to be the same as the sum of the values of its parts*' (p. 79). There is 'great intrinsic value' in 'consciousness of a beautiful object', for example, which is 'a whole', made up of the object and **consciousness** of it (p. 79). The beautiful object appears to have 'little value', if no one is 'conscious of it', but consciousness may be part of a whole that is 'indifferent', as when its object is a neutral one, so it does not always give 'great value' to the whole of which it is part (pp. 79–80). Whatever its 'intrinsic value', consciousness does not always afford a whole 'a value proportioned to the sum of its value and that of its object' (p. 80). Here we have 'a whole possessing a different intrinsic value from the sum of that of its parts' (p. 80).

19 Two especially noteworthy points are **(1)** existence of 'any such part' is a 'necessary condition' of the good of 'the whole', and 'the same language' will also 'express the relation' between 'the good thing' and 'a means' to it; but an 'important difference' is that the part (but not the means) is 'a part of the good thing', of which 'its existence is a necessary condition', whereas 'the necessity' of the 'means to it' is just 'causal' (p. 80). Thus, the means lacks 'intrinsic value', but the 'good in question' cannot exist without the part, and so the 'necessity' connecting them is 'independent of **natural law**' (p. 81). However **(2)**, the part '*itself*' may have no more intrinsic value than 'the means', which is the '**paradox**' of this relation (p. 81). Although, 'existence of the whole', which 'includes the existence of the part', has intrinsic value, the '**inference**' that the part also does would be as 'false' as concluding that, because 'the number of two stones was two, each of the stones was also two' (p. 81).

20   This 'peculiar relation between part and whole' lacks, but requires, a name, and the term, '**organic unity**', might usefully be applied to it (p. 82).

21   **(1)** The parts of the human body are such that one's 'continued existence' is a 'necessary condition' of another's (p. 83). They are 'an "organic unity"', having a '**mutual causal dependence** on one another' and being '**mutually means and ends to one another**' (p. 83). But neither of two mutually dependent things may have 'intrinsic value', or only one may (p. 83). Further, 'the whole cannot be an end to any of its parts' (p. 83). We tend to 'contrast' the whole to 'one of its parts', when we 'mean only *the rest* of the parts'; but, the whole includes 'all its parts', while no part can 'be a cause of the whole', as it 'cannot be a cause of itself' (p. 83). **(2)** When we say that 'the parts' of our body are 'means to the whole', we may be saying that it, 'as a whole', has greater 'value' than the 'sum of values of its parts' (pp. 83–4). But 'the relation' of 'part and whole' is not the same as that between 'part and part', as when we say that one 'could not exist' without the other (p. 84). Unlike the latter, the former 'cannot be causally connected', while their 'relation' may exist, even if the 'parts are not causally connected', as in the 'parts of a picture' (p. 84). So, to say a whole is 'organic', because 'its parts are (in this

sense) "means"' to it, is not to say it is 'organic because its parts are causally dependent on one another' (p. 84).

22 **(3)** A common use of the term '**organic whole**' is to indicate that, just as the whole would not be 'what it is' without the parts, the same would be true of the parts without the whole; and that the whole is 'a part' of its parts; but this is '**self-contradictory**' (p. 84). Part is not related 'to whole' as 'whole to part': no 'part contains analytically the whole to which it belongs', or any other parts of it (p. 85). This false '**doctrine**', that a part can have 'no meaning or significance apart from its whole', shows **Hegel**'s influence on '**modern philosophy**' (p. 85). It is 'easy to see' how it has arisen (p. 85). **(a)** A part's *'existence'* may have a 'natural or causal' connection with 'other parts of its whole', and, when no longer part of the whole, may retain 'the same name' (p. 85). A 'dead arm' is still called an arm, but it is not the same thing as one still 'part of the body'; and so people may say that the latter would not be 'what it is', unless it were 'such a part' (p. 86). But the dead arm was never part of the body, and so is 'only *partially* **identical**' with the living one (p. 86). Here is a case of something that is at one point part, but then not part, of the 'presumed organic whole' (p. 86). It is not that 'properties' of the living arm, which the dead one lacks, exist in it in 'changed form'; they do not 'exist there *at all*' (p. 86). **(b)** A 'different fallacy' is indicated by saying that, without its body, a living arm lacks 'meaning', which suggests having 'importance', being valuable as means or end (p. 86). We might say an arm has value, '*as* a part of the body', but none '*by itself*'; but its value 'does not belong to *it*': value, as a part, is to have no value, only to be 'a part' of something that has (p. 86). This way of thinking leads to the 'assumption' that a thing differs, 'as a part', from what it would otherwise be, giving rise to the 'self-contradictory belief' that it 'may be two different things', but is only 'truly what it is' in one of these 'forms' (p. 87). So, I shall limit use of the term 'organic' to a whole having 'an intrinsic value different in amount from the sum of the values of its parts', but will not imply 'any causal relation' between these parts; that they are 'inconceivable' otherwise than as parts; or that they have a different value as parts (p. 87). This relation of 'organic whole' to parts is crucially important in ethics, which is concerned with comparing 'the relative values of various goods'; but most serious errors arise, if it is thought that a whole's value is just 'the sum of the values' of its parts (p. 87).

23 In conclusion, (1): ethics' particular role is not investigation of 'human conduct', but of that 'property of things which is denoted by the term "good"' (p. 87). (2) This is 'simple and indefinable' (pp. 87–8). (3) Assertions about its 'relation to other things' either state the extent to which things have it, or indicate 'causal relations' between things possessing it and other things (p. 88). (4) A whole may have it 'in a degree different' from what is 'obtained by summing the degrees in which its parts possess it' (p. 88).

Chapter II (pp. 89–110)

Naturalistic Ethics

24 Ethics concerns three questions: 'what is *meant* by good'; 'what things are good in themselves'; and how to 'make what exists in the world as good as possible' (p. 89). I shall now discuss ethical 'theories' which have the common characteristic of committing 'the naturalistic fallacy' (pp. 89–90).

25 There are 'two groups' of such theories (p. 90). In one,

'good' is defined by reference to 'a natural object', which is an 'object of **experience**'; in the other, it is defined in relation to an object in a '**supersensible real world**', and these theories may be called '**metaphysical**' (pp. 90–1). While both commit the 'naturalistic fallacy', it is 'convenient' to distinguish the theories that regard goodness as consisting 'in a relation to something which exists here and now' from those 'which do not' (p. 91). The first group divides into those that maintain that 'pleasure' is the 'sole good' and the rest (p. 91). I shall deal with the latter subgroup in this chapter, and '**Hedonism**' in the next (p. 91).

26   The ethical theories in this chapter claim that 'good' means having a '*natural* property, other than pleasure', and I have called this approach '**Naturalism**' (pp. 91–2). It does not matter what the particular theory asserts 'good' means, it is still a 'naturalistic theory' (p. 92). By 'nature' and 'natural objects', I mean 'the subject-matter of the **natural sciences**' and '**psychology**': all the things that have, do, or will '**exist in time**'; and it is 'easy to say' which objects are, or are not, natural in this sense (pp. 92–3). It is not so simple when it comes to the 'properties' of 'natural objects' (p. 93). I acknowledge that 'good is a property of certain natural objects', but it is not itself 'a natural property', and my 'test', again, is 'existence in time' (p. 93). It is hard to imagine 'good' existing 'by *itself* in time', and not 'merely as a property of some natural object' (p. 93). However, the 'natural properties' of an object seem to exist independently of it, being 'parts' of which the object is composed, not 'mere predicates which attach to it' (p. 93). If removed, 'no object would be left', as they give it its 'substance'; but this is 'not so with good' (p. 93).

27   So, what theories define 'good' by 'reference to' a natural property (p. 93)? **Rousseau** recommends 'life according to

33

nature', and some still argue that we should 'live naturally' (p. 93). But not everything that is 'natural is equally good', and the job of ethics is to provide '**general rules**' to help us 'avoid' bad things, and 'secure' good ones (p. 94). The phrase, 'to live naturally', seems to suggest some 'natural good', which 'Nature' fixes, which could be interpreted in terms of what is the '*normal* state' of a particular organism, as in its being healthy, rather than diseased, although this is also 'natural' (p. 94). But was 'the excellence' of **Socrates** or Shakespeare normal, or 'abnormal, extraordinary' (p. 94)? The latter is 'often better' than the former (pp. 94–5). Even if the 'normal is good', this cannot be regarded as 'obvious'; it is an 'open question' (p. 95). For example, the word 'health', when used to 'denote something good, is good', but this does not show that it is 'also good', when used 'to denote something normal' (p. 95). 'Good' does not 'mean anything that is natural', by definition, and it is an open question whether what 'is natural is good' (p. 95).

28 'Natural' is also used to suggest 'something good', as in 'natural affections', as opposed to 'unnatural crimes and vices' (p. 96). The 'naturalistic reason' here seems to be that 'we cannot improve on nature', and so should regard as good only **acts 'necessary' for 'preservation of life'** (p. 96). But this is another example of the 'naturalistic fallacy' (p. 96). That 'certain acts' are necessary for preserving life is no reason for '*praising* them', or doing only those (p. 96). Undeniably, nature has 'set limits to what is possible', thus limiting the means for 'obtaining what is good' (p. 96). But, when nature is thought to prefer 'what is necessary', this means necessary for achieving 'a certain end', which is 'presupposed as the highest good'; and nature cannot decide what this is (p. 96). Why should we think that what is 'necessary to life' is better

than, for example, what is necessary for studying '**metaphysics**', which may be the only thing that makes life 'worth living' (pp. 96–7)?

29 It is 'certainly fallacious' to claim that something is good '*because* it is "natural"', and bad because it is not (p. 97). Currently, the most popular attempt to '*systematise* an **appeal to nature**' is by applying 'the term "**Evolution**"' to 'ethical questions' (p. 97). The contention is that evolution shows us, not only how we are, but how 'we *ought* to develop' (p. 97). **Spencer**'s writings provide an example of 'the naturalistic fallacy as used in support of **Evolutionist Ethics**' (p. 98).

30 This arises from **Darwin**'s theory about how certain animal species 'became established', while others did not: that the former had characteristics that enabled them to survive in their 'environment' (pp. 98–9). This '**Natural Selection**', or '**survival of the fittest**', lends itself, particularly in view of the evolution of human beings, to the idea of movement from 'lower' to 'higher' (p. 99). But Darwin's theory is about what causes 'certain biological effects', and argues that 'survival' is of the 'fittest to survive', not of the 'fittest to fulfil a good purpose' (p. 99).

31 But Spencer argues that ethics' concern is with 'universal conduct' in the 'last stages of its evolution', when it '*gains ethical sanction*' by becoming 'less militant' and more co-operative (p. 100). He appears to be influenced by the view that 'better' means 'more evolved', and thus commits the 'naturalistic fallacy' (pp. 100–1). He seems unaware of the fact that 'more evolved' is not the same as 'better', and that the proposition that the former is also the latter needs to be proved (p. 101).

32 He is not consistent; he argues that what is more evolved is also better, then 'recommends' an 'utterly different' view: that such a 'conclusion' would be *'false'* unless it is true that life is *'pleasant* on the whole' (p. 101). So, he emerges as 'a Hedonist', not 'an **Evolutionist**': our 'degree of evolution' serves merely as a *'criterion* **of ethical value'**, and can only be shown to be that by proving that 'the more evolved is always, on the whole, the pleasanter' (p. 102).

33 He argues that nobody, whether 'pessimist' or 'optimist', can 'avoid taking for the ultimate moral aim a desirable state of feeling', which may be called, 'enjoyment' or 'happiness'; but what is 'the relation of Pleasure and Evolution' (pp. 102–3)? By this, he should mean that pleasure is the *'only* intrinsically desirable thing'; that other things are 'good', only insofar as they are 'means to its existence'; and that 'more evolved conduct' is better than the 'less evolved', because it provides more pleasure (p. 103). However, he then tells us that there are 'two conditions' that prove more evolved conduct better: that it should 'produce more life' and that this should 'contain a balance of pleasure' (p. 103). But, while producing more life is one way of providing more pleasure, it is not the only one: a small amount might yield a 'greater quantity of pleasure', leading us, on the 'hedonistic supposition', to prefer 'less evolved conduct' (pp. 103–4). As Spencer seems to argue that the larger of 'two quantities' of life that produce equal amounts of pleasure is 'preferable' to the lesser one, he appears to be saying that the 'degree of evolution' is an 'ultimate condition of value', and so to adhere to both the 'Evolutionistic proposition' and the 'Hedonistic' one (p. 104). But why does he think it 'self-evident that life is good or bad', according to whether or not it produces 'a surplus of agreeable feeling' (p. 104)? His 'proof' is that it 'creates absurdities' to apply the word, 'good', to conduct that produces a balance of 'painful' consequences, which suggests the naturalistic fallacy: that 'pleasant' is 'the very meaning' of 'good' (pp. 104–5). And '**naturalistic Hedonism**' is implied in his view that 'virtue' can be defined only 'in terms of happiness': he seems to assume that 'we *must* mean by good conduct what is productive of pleasure' (p. 105). His 'main view', that 'pleasure is the sole good', and that the 'direction of evolution' is the best indicator of how to 'get most of it', would be, if he could prove that quantity of pleasure is always in 'direct proportion' to degree of evolution, a 'valuable contribution' to '**Sociology**'; but it will not tell us 'why one way of acting should be considered better than another' (pp. 105–6).

34 I shall restrict the term, 'Evolutionistic Ethics', to the view that 'the tendency of "evolution"' shows us the way 'we *ought* to go' (p. 106). It should not be confused with such views as: the way 'living things' have developed is, as a matter of fact, 'also better'; Spencer's 'main view' that the 'more evolved', though 'not itself the better', is a *'criterion'* of it; or that, while evolution does not show us what will be the best results of 'our efforts', it does show us what it is *'possible'* to achieve and the means of doing so (pp. 106–7). Evolutionistic ethics is the 'fallacious view' that 'good simply *means* the side on which Nature is working', so we should go in the 'direction of evolution' (p. 108). But 'Darwin's **theory of natural selection**' states a natural law only in the sense that, 'given certain conditions', certain results always follow (p. 108). Under other conditions, this might produce, 'not a development from lower to higher', but the opposite, which might involve human beings' 'extinction' (pp. 108–9). If we realized that there is no evidence for believing 'Nature' is always 'on the side of the Good', we might be less inclined to believe that we do not need evidence for this belief, or that evolution has something to 'say to Ethics' (p. 109).

37

35   In this chapter, I have criticized views that identify the 'simple notion which we mean by "good" with some other notion' (p. 109). One typical 'naturalistic' view is to approve 'what is "natural"' (p. 110). However, 'natural' might mean 'normal' or 'necessary', neither of which is 'always good' (p. 110). 'Evolutionistic Ethics' is a 'more important' such theory, and study of Spencer's theory shows it to be based on the 'fallacious opinion that to be "better" means to be "more evolved"' (p. 110).

Chapter III (pp. 111–60)

Hedonism

36   This chapter concerns 'the most widely held of all ethical principles': that only pleasure 'is good' (p. 111). This view's prevalence is due to the 'naturalistic fallacy': that pleasure seems to be 'involved in the *definition* of "good"' (p. 111). However, 'of all hedonistic writers', only Sidgwick has realized that 'good' means 'something unanalysable', and that hedonism's truth must be based 'solely on its self-evidence' (p. 111). Belief that pleasure is 'the sole good' is a 'mere *intuition*' (p. 111). But we can see why pleasure has this 'unique position', as it is hard to distinguish what 'we are pleased with' from what 'we *approve*'; and easy to believe that, '"I think this is good" is identical with, "I am pleased with this"' (pp. 112–13). The naturalistic fallacy also involves failure to distinguish 'the proposition, "This is good"', from others, 'which seem to resemble it' (p. 113).

37   Hedonism is 'a form of Naturalism' and, to be absolutely clear, the view I am criticizing is that pleasure '*alone* is good as an end or in itself' (pp. 113–14). I do not quarrel

with the view that pleasure *'is* good as an end or in itself', or any views about the 'best means' of securing pleasure 'or any other end' (p. 114). Further, I do not disagree with most hedonists' 'practical conclusions' about how life should be conducted, only with 'the reasons' with which they support them (p. 114).

38 Hedonists think that everything other than pleasure is 'only good as means to pleasure', or for its sake (p. 115). This view has been maintained by 'Utilitarians', such as Bentham and Mill and, to show its 'confusions and inconsistencies', I shall first examine 'Mill's doctrine', as stated in his *Utilitarianism*, and then 'consider and refute' Sidgwick's more 'precise conceptions and arguments' (pp. 115–16). Two key points will emerge from this discussion: that the naturalistic fallacy must be avoided, and that 'means and ends' need to be clearly distinguished (p. 116).

39 Mill's book discusses 'many ethical principles' in a 'clear and fair' way, but my concern is with his 'mistakes' in relation to the '**Hedonistic principle**' (p. 116). Having defined 'happiness' as 'pleasure, and the absence of pain', he says that they are 'the only things desirable as ends' (pp. 116–17). Thus, 'happiness is desirable, and *the only thing desirable*, as an end'; other things are 'only desirable as means to that end' (p. 117). He also tells us (and I agree) that '**Questions of ultimate ends** are not amenable to direct proof', and that 'Questions about ends' concern 'what things are desirable' (p. 117). Thus, Mill uses 'desirable' or 'desirable as an end' as 'equivalent to the words "good as an end"' (p. 117). What reasons does he give for his view that 'pleasure alone is good as an end' (p. 117)?

40 He argues that, just as the only proof that a thing is 'visible' is that 'people actually see it', the only evidence that 'anything is desirable' is that 'people do actually desire it' (p. 118). The only reason that can be given why 'the general happiness is desirable' is that 'each person, so far as he believes it to be attainable, desires his own happiness' (p. 118). But this (he goes on) is 'all the proof' required that 'happiness is a good'; that 'each person's happiness is a good to that person'; and that 'the general happiness' is a good to 'the aggregate of all persons' (p. 118). But this is so 'naïve' a use of the naturalistic fallacy that it is 'wonderful how Mill failed to see it' (p. 118). 'Desirable' does not mean 'able to be desired', but 'what *ought* to be desired' (p. 118). 'Desirable' does mean 'what it is good to desire' but, once this is understood, we cannot say that our 'only test' of this is 'what is actually desired' (p. 119). If it were, it would not be possible to speak, as in the **'Prayer Book'**, of '*good* desires' (p. 119). Indeed, Mill refers to a 'better and nobler object of desire', as if 'what is desired were not *ipso facto* good, and good in proportion to the amount it is desired' (p. 119).

41 Mill has tried to 'establish the identity of good' by confusing 'the proper sense of "desirable"' with what it would mean, if it were 'analogous to', for example, 'visible' (p. 119). Once he thinks he has established that 'the good means the desired', he realizes that, to show (as he wishes) that 'pleasure alone is good', he must prove that only it 'is really desired': what Sidgwick calls **'Psychological Hedonism'** (pp. 119–20).

42 We shall take it that pleasure is the 'object of all desire' and 'the universal end of all human activity', but people seem to desire other things, such as 'money, approbation, fame' (p. 120). To 'justify Hedonism', there must a 'necessary or universal relation' between 'desire' and 'pleasure' (p. 120). There is, but it does not support hedonism. Hedonists maintain that pleasure is 'always the object of desire', but I believe it is (partly, anyway) its '*cause*' (p. 120). I desire 'a glass of port';

the idea of drinking it is 'before my mind', even though I am not drinking it (p. 121). How does pleasure come into this? I believe the '*idea*' of drinking the port produces 'a feeling of pleasure in my mind', leading to what is called 'desire': I desire the wine, because of my feeling of pleasure (p. 121). However, Mill argues that, when I desire the port, I do not desire it, but the pleasure 'I expect to get from it' (p. 121). So, Mill holds that 'the idea of a pleasure *not actual* is always necessary to cause desire'; I maintain that 'the *actual* pleasure caused by the idea of something else' is 'always necessary to cause desire' (p. 121). 'Psychological Hedonism' confuses a 'pleasant thought' with the 'thought of a pleasure'; and only when we have the latter can pleasure 'be said to be the *object* of desire' (pp. 121–2). When we have only a 'pleasant thought', the 'object of the thought', such as the port, is 'the object of desire' (p. 122). If we agree that 'pleasure is always the cause of desire', we must reject the 'ethical doctrine that pleasure alone is good': pleasure is not 'what I desire', but something I have 'before I can want anything' (pp. 122–3).

43 Mill has another argument for happiness being 'the sole end of human action' (p. 123). He acknowledges that people desire things other than pleasure, such as 'virtue' and 'money', appearing to contradict his view that 'pleasure is the only thing desirable, because it is the only thing desired' (p. 123). How does he get round this? By saying that when something like money is desired 'in and for' itself, it is desired only 'as a part of happiness' (p. 123). However, he also says it is 'only desirable as a means to happiness' (p. 123). But, if it is 'only desirable as a means', how can it also be 'desirable as an end-in-itself' (pp. 123–4)? Mill's answer is that 'what is only a means to an end, is the same thing as a part of that end' (p. 124). Mill has had to eliminate the 'distinction between means and ends', due to failure to 'distinguish "end" in the sense of what is desirable, from "end" in the sense of what is desired' (p. 124).

44 Mill's 'fundamental propositions' are that to consider an object 'desirable' and 'pleasant' are 'one and the same thing', and that it is a 'physical and metaphysical impossibility' to desire a thing, 'except in proportion as the idea of it is pleasant' (p. 124). The first one is based on the naturalistic fallacy, the second on a confusion of 'ends and means' and of 'a pleasant thought with the thought of pleasure' (p. 124).

Thus, for Mill, 'the desirable', which he uses as 'a synonym for "the good"', means 'what *can* be desired', the 'test' of this being 'what actually is desired' (p. 124). If (he says) we can find a thing that is 'always and alone desired', it will 'necessarily' be the only 'desirable' thing, and the only thing 'good as an end' (p. 124). Use of the naturalistic fallacy here is obvious. Mill takes 'good' to mean 'what is desired': and this can be 'defined in natural terms' (p. 125). He is saying 'we ought to desire' a thing, because we 'do desire it' (p. 125). But, if 'ought to desire' means only 'do desire', he can only say that we 'desire so and so, because we do desire it', which is a 'mere **tautology**', not an 'ethical proposition' (p. 125). I have already shown Mill's claim that we 'never desire anything but pleasure' to be wrong, by pointing out the 'confusion' between the 'cause of desire' and its 'object' (p. 125). We may only have a desire, if we first experience 'some *actual* pleasure', but this does not mean that the object of our desire is 'some *future* pleasure' (p. 125). Lastly, he accepts we do desire 'other things than pleasure', but claims we actually 'desire nothing else'; and seeks to 'explain away' the contradiction through confusion of means and ends (p. 126).

45 But, even though Mill's 'naturalistic arguments for

Hedonism' can be refuted, the proposition that 'pleasure alone is desirable' could 'still be true' (p. 126). It belongs to 'the class of **first principles**', which are incapable of 'direct proof' but, in relation to which (as Mill 'rightly says'), 'considerations' may be put forward that can lead the 'the intellect' to accept or reject them (p. 126). This makes ethical hedonism's 'fundamental proposition' what Sidgwick calls an '**object of intuition**': which his intuition 'affirms', but mine 'denies' (p. 126). Talk of 'considerations', not 'proof', may seem 'unsatisfactory', but is it unsatisfactory because of absence of proof or lack of agreement (p. 127)? I think it is the latter. There are many things we cannot prove, such as 'this is a chair', but that does not make us uneasy (p. 127). We all agree 'it is a chair', and are 'content' (p. 127). Indeed, 'who can prove that proof itself is a warrant of truth' (p. 127)? It is invariably 'disagreement', not the 'impossibility of proof', that makes us regard a state of affairs as 'unsatisfactory' (p. 127). We should not worry if 'we cannot prove whether pleasure alone is good or not' (p. 127). It may be possible to reach agreement about it, which will be enough. By exploring all the implications of 'the fundamental principle of Hedonism', I shall attempt to secure agreement that it is 'very like an absurdity' (p. 128). But, given the complexity of 'philosophical questions', no more than 'limited assent' may be possible (p. 128).

46 Discussion of '**Intuitionistic Hedonism**' will involve a change in 'my ethical method' (p. 128). Hitherto, I have argued something that can be proved: that 'good is indefinable', and that denying it 'involves a fallacy' (p. 128). Now, my concern is with 'what things' are good, where 'direct proof' is impossible (p. 128). The best I can hope for is what Mill calls 'indirect proof' (p. 128). The 'intuition' to be 'submitted to our verdict' is that 'pleasure alone is good as an end' (pp. 128–9).

43

47 What about another of Mill's views: 'difference of quality in pleasures' (p. 129)? Bentham based his argument for hedonism on ' "**quantity of pleasure**" alone', holding that 'quantity of pleasure being equal, pushpin is as good as poetry'; but Mill regards '**quality of pleasure**' as a 'different ground for estimating pleasures' (p. 129). 'Of two pleasures' (he writes), the one experts (those who have experienced both) prefer, is the 'more desirable', as it is superior 'in quality' (p. 129). But Mill's acceptance of a qualitative difference in pleasures is either 'inconsistent with his Hedonism', or affords no other basis for it than 'mere quantity of pleasure' (p. 130). He maintains that it is 'the same thing' to consider a thing 'desirable' and 'pleasant' (p. 130). So, the 'preference of experts' can only prove that 'one pleasure is pleasanter than another' (p. 130). But how does this differ from 'the standard of quantity of pleasure' (p. 130)? If there is this difference of quality, 'the basis of Mill's Hedonism collapses', because he is accepting that one thing may be 'preferred over another', and so 'proved more desirable', although 'it is not more desired' (p. 130). This being so, 'Mill's judgment of preference is just a judgment of that intuitional kind which I have been contending to be necessary to establish the hedonistic or any other principle', and is an admission that 'good is good and indefinable' (p. 130).

48 Mill's claim that experts should judge whether 'one pleasure is more desirable than another' has a further implication (p. 131). If pleasures can differ qualitatively, they must be 'complex', consisting of pleasure and what 'produces' it (p. 131). To say '**sensual indulgence**' is 'lower than another pleasure', despite equal quantity of pleasure, is to accept that things may be 'good, or bad', 'independently' of their accompanying pleasure; but, if pleasure is the only good, there must

44

be something 'common to all different "pleasures"', which may be present in 'different degrees', but which 'cannot differ in *kind*' (pp. 131–2). Introducing 'quality of pleasure' means it cannot be claimed that 'pleasure *alone* is good as an end': there must be something '*not* present in all pleasures' that is '*also* good as an end' (p. 132). The 'hedonistic principle' that only pleasure is good is incompatible with 'the view that one pleasure may be of a better quality than another' (p. 132). We must choose between them.

49 Sidgwick rejects 'the test by quality of pleasure', embracing the 'hedonistic principle' (p. 132). I shall examine his arguments, in the hope of showing that there are some we can reject.

50 In his *Methods of Ethics*, Sidgwick argues that, if we examine what is 'commonly judged to be good', it appears that nothing possesses this 'quality', unless it has some 'relation to human existence' or 'consciousness': if there is 'any Good other than Happiness to be sought by man, as an ultimate practical end, it can only be the Goodness, Perfection, or Excellence of Human Existence' (pp. 133–4). But is this 'justified' (p. 135)? I think not. Imagine two very different worlds, one 'exceedingly beautiful', the other the 'ugliest' possible, neither of which could be inhabited, or even seen, by human beings (p. 135). Would it be 'irrational' to prefer the beautiful world to exist (p. 135)? If not, Sidgwick's 'principle' crumbles, because this is to admit that it is 'better in itself' for a beautiful thing to exist than an ugly one, 'quite apart from its effects on any human feeling': which means we must 'include in our ultimate end something beyond the limits of human existence' (p. 136).

51 But Sidgwick has 'limited the ultimate end' to 'parts of Human Existence' (p. 136). Which parts? Some (he observes)

45

may regard 'contemplation of Beauty' or 'Free or Virtuous action' as 'preferable' to pleasure, but he asks us to exercise our 'intuitive judgment' about the matter, and then examine the ordinary 'judgments of mankind' (p. 137). He believes the first will indicate that such objects are not 'intrinsically desirable', without any 'relation to conscious existence'; we consider them important, because they promote 'the happiness of sentient beings' (p. 137). The second will show these objects produce pleasure, and are approved to the extent that they promote 'general happiness' (p. 138). Even the value attached to knowledge reflects its 'fruitfulness' (p. 138). Again, although the 'main aim' of our 'ordinary moral discourse' is to promote each other's 'virtuous impulses', we accept there can be too much 'cultivation of virtue', leading to 'neglect' of 'other conditions of happiness'; thus, what promotes 'general happiness' should be the 'criterion' for determining the degree to which virtue is cultivated (pp. 138–9). So, 'Pleasure alone is good for its own sake'; everything else is good only as 'a means' to it (p. 139).

52   Pleasure is something 'of which we may be conscious', and from which it can be distinguished; but is it 'valuable in itself', or only when we are conscious of it (p. 139)? This point is brought out in **Plato**'s *Philebus*, in which Socrates persuades **Protarchus** that 'Hedonism is absurd', by showing that it involves regarding pleasure as 'good as an end', irrespective of whether or not 'we are conscious of it' (pp. 139–40). A person could lead a life of 'the greatest pleasure', even though he lacked 'intelligence and memory and knowledge' (p. 140). Can anyone really believe such a position to be 'reasonable', and that 'pleasure alone is good as an end' (p. 140)? But, if pleasure is 'comparatively valueless' without consciousness of it, we have to say that pleasure is '*not* the only end', and that

46

at least 'some consciousness' must be 'included with it', as 'part of the end' (p. 141). This is not to say that the *practical* conclusions' of the utilitarians, as to how we should live, are wrong; but 'their *reason*' for holding them, that 'pleasure alone is good', certainly is (p. 141).

53 So, either pleasure alone is 'desirable', or 'consciousness of it' is 'more desirable still' (p. 142). Both 'propositions cannot be true' and, as the latter clearly is, 'pleasure is *not* the sole good' (p. 142). It could be argued that this does not harm hedonism, as hedonists have always meant 'consciousness of pleasure', not simply pleasure, though they have not said so (p. 142). But I do not believe that 'even consciousness of pleasure' is 'the sole good', for the 'same method' that shows this to be 'more valuable' than pleasure also appears to show that it is 'less valuable than other things' (p. 142). To find the 'degree of value a thing has in itself', we need to strip out its 'usual accompaniments', as we did with pleasure (p. 142).

54 Sidgwick says our ordinary, common-sense judgements about things that might be thought to share 'the attribute of goodness' with pleasure are related to 'the degree' to which these things produce pleasure (p. 143). But this only shows that pleasure is 'a good *criterion* of right action': that conduct that produces most pleasure also produces 'most good on the whole' (p. 143). We are not entitled to conclude that 'the greatest pleasure *constituted* what was best on the whole'; it leaves 'open the alternative' that the 'greatest quantity of pleasure' is, in general, 'accompanied by the greatest quantity of *other goods*', and so pleasure is '*not* the sole good' (p. 143). What Sidgwick tends to show is that something is 'not held to be good, unless it gives a balance of pleasure', not that approval of it is 'in proportion to the quantity of pleasure' (p. 143).

55 Sidgwick contends that regarding happiness as only

'part of Ultimate Good' does not accord with 'the facts of intuition' (p. 144). However, taking the example of 'the enjoyment of Beauty', the fact that there is 'much value' in this, and 'none in the mere contemplation of it', does not mean that 'all the value' belongs to the other constituent of 'that complex fact', the pleasure (p. 144). We are not entitled to conclude that, because there is no value in 'one part of a whole, considered by itself', all the value lies in the other part: *both* the pleasure *and* the contemplation' may be equally necessary parts of 'the good' (p. 144). Sidgwick ignores what I have called 'the **principle of "organic relations"**' (p. 144). His argument is misleading, because he considers that, if a 'whole state' is valuable, but one part of it has no value, *'by itself'*, the other part, by itself, must have 'all the value' of the whole (p. 144). But, if the whole is 'organic', the other part may also be valueless in isolation, or the whole may have 'much greater' value (pp. 144–5). All the parts need to be considered *'in isolation'*, but Sidgwick does so only with one, failing to ask whether, if pleasure 'existed absolutely by itself', it would possess much value (p. 145). As pleasure appears to be a 'necessary constituent of most valuable wholes', it is all too easy to conclude that, as the other constituents seem to lack value by themselves, all the value lies in it (p. 145). Even if Sidgwick is right that 'consciousness of pleasure' is more valuable than 'Contemplation of Beauty', I maintain that 'pleasurable Contemplation of Beauty' is more valuable still (p. 145). It certainly cannot be maintained that even consciousness of pleasure is 'the *sole* good' (p. 145).

56 Another point makes it even clearer that a pleasurable whole's value is not 'solely' due to 'the pleasure' it contains (pp. 145–6). Sidgwick holds that, in our ordinary, common-sense judgements of things, approval is in 'proportion' to the degree to which they promote pleasure (p. 146). But this 'doubtful' contention only has any credibility when all the *'consequences'* of particular states are considered: that is, when they are viewed as a means (p. 146). When judging things as ends, not means, people often prefer 'less pleasant' to more pleasant 'states', agreeing with Mill that there are 'higher pleasures' that are 'more valuable' (p. 146). For example, it is the general view that 'the lowest forms of sexual enjoyment' are 'positively bad', even though they may be 'the most pleasant states we ever experience' (p. 146).

57   So, to be conscious only of pleasure, 'however great the quantity', would not be 'very desirable' (p. 147). What are desirable are 'many complicated states of mind', combining consciousness of pleasure with that 'of other things' (p. 147). Recognition of the 'principle of organic unities' enables us to see that consciousness of pleasure is 'not the sole good', and that other states, of which it is part, are 'much better' (p. 147). Thus, hedonism is refuted.

58   'Egoism' is a 'form of Hedonism', which holds that we should each 'pursue our own greatest happiness as our ultimate end' (p. 147). But the term sometimes denotes a view which holds that aiming at our own pleasure is the 'best *means* to the ultimate end': whether that be 'our own greatest pleasure or not' (p. 148). This latter kind of egoist may maintain that, by pursuing his own pleasure, he will be 'most likely to increase the general sum of happiness' (p. 148).

59   The first type of egoism, which is at the root of '**Hobbes**' Ethics', is 'not much held' today (p. 148). This type of egoist is not necessarily a hedonist. When the 'plain man' says that what promotes 'his own interest' is the only possible 'justification' for his 'actions', he means 'advancement', not 'pleasure' (p. 149). But what does it mean to say that a thing is 'good *for me*' (p. 150)? It must be 'the thing' or 'possession of

it', not its *'goodness'*, which cannot just 'belong to me' (p. 150).
My only reason for pursuing 'my own good' is that it is *'good absolutely* that I should have something which, if I have it,
others cannot' (p. 150). If a person's '"interest" or "happiness"'
is his 'sole ultimate end', it must be *'the sole good, the* **Universal
Good***'*, and thus 'the only thing that anybody ought to aim at'
(p. 150). What egoism holds is that *'each* man's happiness is
the sole good', making each of 'a number of different things'
the 'only good thing', which is an 'absolute contradiction'
(pp. 150–1).

60   Sidgwick says 'Egoism is rational' (p. 151). But can
something be 'an ultimate rational end for one person and
not for another' (p. 151)? To be 'an ultimate rational end', a
thing must be 'truly good in itself', a 'part of Universal Good'
(p. 151). So, either the 'Egoist's happiness' is 'good in itself,
and so a part of Universal Good', or it is not 'good in itself at
all' (p. 151). But if the latter, what would be the point of the egoist aiming at it? A thing cannot be good only for one person; it
would not be 'a rational end for him', as it would not be 'truly
good in itself': the 'phrase "an ultimate rational end for him-
self is a contradiction in terms"' (p. 151). Indeed, egoism leads
to the 'fundamental contradiction' that 'an immense number
of different things are, *each* of them, the *sole* good' (p. 152).
But there is nothing to show that, if one person's 'happiness is
desirable', it is not 'part of Universal Good' and, if it is a 'good
thing', then 'everyone else has an equal reason to pursue it'
(pp. 152–3). Additions like 'for him' or 'for me' to 'ultimate
rational end' and 'good' just cause 'confusion' (p. 153). The
'only possible' justification for any action is to obtain 'the
greatest possible amount of what is good absolutely' (p. 153).
When someone claims pursuit of his own happiness as justification for his actions, this can only mean that this is how he

can achieve 'the greatest possible amount of Universal Good' (p. 153).

61   Sidgwick addresses what he calls the 'profoundest problem of Ethics': how to reconcile 'the **maxim of Prudence**' (pursuit of individual happiness as 'an end') with 'the **principle of Rational Benevolence**' (the '**Utilitarian Duty**' to promote general happiness) (p. 153). Belief in **God** (he suggests) would 'ensure' it, as his '**Sanctions**' would make it 'every one's interest' to promote it (p. 154). But what is he seeking from '**Divine Omnipotence**': that 'what gives other people pleasure' should also give it to the individual (p. 154)? This is the 'characteristic fallacy of **Empiricism**': to think that changing the facts can remove 'a contradiction' (p. 154). The 'principle of Egoism', that '*each* man's happiness should be the *sole good*', is 'in itself a contradiction'; that of **Universalistic Hedonism**', that 'the Happiness of all is the *sole good*', would just create another (p. 155). He confuses it with 'the mere fact' that 'our own greatest happiness', and 'that of all', are not 'always attainable by the same means' (p. 155). The fact is that 'in this world the quantity of good' achievable is 'ridiculously small compared to that which is imaginable' (p. 155). All Sidgwick's 'profoundest problem' amounts to, is that when we secure 'as much good as possible in one place', we secure less, 'on the whole', due to the 'quantity of attainable good' being 'limited' (p. 155). It is a '**false antithesis**' to say my choice is between 'my own good and that of *all*'; it is 'between my own and that of *others*' (p. 155).

62   The 'doctrine of Egoism is self-contradictory', and it is present in 'the transition from Naturalistic Hedonism' to 'Utilitarianism' (p. 155). Mill believes he can infer the 'happiness of all is the good of all' from 'Each man's happiness is his own good' (p. 156). However, a correct understanding of 'his own good' shows that the former 'can only be inferred from "The happiness of all is the good of each"' (p. 156).

63 But, 'Egoism', in the form being discussed, is sometimes thought 'reasonable', as it is confused with 'Egoism as a doctrine of means' (p. 156). And as we are in 'an imperfect state', we sometimes ought to do what is 'good only or chiefly as means': which may be pursuit of our 'own pleasure' (pp. 156–7). We must do 'the best we can': what is 'absolutely "right"', but not 'absolutely good' (p. 157).

64 The 'chief reason' for 'adopting the name "Utilitarianism"' was to indicate that 'right and wrong conduct must be judged by its results', and that right conduct should 'promote the *interest* of everybody'; it then came to be held that 'actions are to be judged' by the extent to which 'they are a means to *pleasure*' (p. 157). A tendency of utilitarians is to think of everything as 'mere means', and to overlook the fact that some things that are 'good as means are also good as ends' (pp. 157–8). They tend to regard current pleasures as 'a means' to future ones, judging them by their 'consequences', rather than valuing them in themselves (p. 158).

Utilitarians talk of 'the greatest happiness of the greatest number' but, if pleasure is 'the sole good', given its quantity is 'equally great', it should not matter how many people enjoy it; so, they should only be aiming at 'the existence of pleasure in a great number of persons' as the 'best *means*' of securing 'the greatest quantity of pleasure' (p. 158). But they do not seem to distinguish pleasure, and 'consciousness' of it, from its 'possession by a person' (p. 158). If we 'take the Utilitarian principle strictly', to mean that many people having pleasure is 'good in itself', it is not the 'hedonistic' principle, and includes 'more than mere pleasure' as a 'necessary part of the ultimate end' (p. 158). What can be said in its favour is that, as a matter of 'empirical fact', acting in ways that bring 'most good' also generally brings 'most pleasure' (p. 159). But I have shown that 'many complex states of mind' are 'more valuable than the pleasure they contain', so '*no form of Hedonism can be true*', while the 'practical guidance' pleasure gives, 'as a *criterion*', is 'very doubtful' (p. 159).

65 The 'prevalence' of hedonism is due to the naturalistic fallacy (p. 159). Mill 'commits' this, and is also wrong to believe that pleasure is the only 'object of desire' (p. 160). His acceptance of qualitatively 'inferior' pleasures suggests it is an intuition, but a 'false one' (p. 160). Sidgwick does not distinguish pleasure from consciousness of it, but the latter is not the 'sole good' (p. 160). 'Egoism' and 'Utilitarianism', the 'main types of Hedonism', contradict each other, as they claim different things to be the '*sole* good', but Sidgwick fails to note this (p. 160).

Chapter IV (pp. 161–91)

Metaphysical Ethics

66 Philosophers like **Kant** hold that 'ethical truths' follow from 'metaphysical' ones (p. 161). 'Metaphysicians' recognize that 'not everything which *is* is a "natural object"', and are concerned with the objects that 'do not exist in time', and 'in fact, do not *exist* at all' (p. 161). As only good things, 'not *goodness*', can exist in time, this is the 'class' to which what we mean by 'the adjective "good"' belongs (p. 161). However, while metaphysicians' main 'contribution' to philosophy has been to draw attention to 'the importance of objects which do not exist', they have not 'recognised this', maintaining that what does not exist 'in time', must '*exist* elsewhere': that

53

what does not exist 'in Nature' exists in 'some supersensible reality' (p. 162). So, I define metaphysics 'by a reference to supersensible *reality*' (p. 163).

67   A 'Metaphysical Ethics' is characterized by the claim that what 'would be perfectly good' exists, but is 'not natural' (p. 164). Kant claims this, when he says 'his "**Kingdom of Ends**" is the ideal'; and such 'ethical principles', unlike 'Naturalism', do recognize that more is needed for 'perfect goodness' than 'what exists here and now' (p. 164). But metaphysicians claim that ethical propositions follow from metaphysical ones: that what is 'real' has some 'logical bearing' on what is 'good', and that 'knowledge of supersensible reality' is required '*as a premise* for correct conclusions as to what ought to exist' (pp. 164–5). However, the view that propositions about what is good can be inferred from ones about the nature of reality commits 'the naturalistic fallacy' (p. 165). A truth about what is 'good in itself' is 'unique in kind', and cannot be 'reduced to any assertion about reality' (p. 165).

68   What 'bearing' could 'the nature of supersensible reality' have on ethics (p. 166)? There are two kinds of ethical question: what 'ought to be?' and what 'ought we to do?'; and the nature of supersensible reality could be relevant to the latter, which concerns '**practical Ethics**' (p. 166). If metaphysics could show 'we are immortal', and how present conduct affects our future 'condition', that would influence our views of what 'we ought to do' (p. 166). But many metaphysical 'doctrines' tell us, not about 'a future reality', but an '**eternal**' one, said to be the only 'real' thing, and one our actions cannot affect: from this, it follows that we can never 'bring any good to pass', so there can be nothing 'we ought to do' (pp. 166–7). Propositions about what we 'ought to do' can only be 'consistent with the Metaphysics of an eternal reality', if **(1)** it is not the '*only* true reality': a 'moral rule', requiring us to achieve a 'certain end', can only be 'justified', if there is some possibility of its being attained; our 'efforts' must be able to achieve 'the *real* existence of some good' to be worth making (p. 167). **(2)** The 'eternal reality' is not 'the sole good', because a 'reasonable rule of conduct' requires that what we are asked to achieve should not only be 'truly real', but also 'truly good' (pp. 167–8). If it does not add to 'the sum of good in the Universe', there is 'no reason' for us to try to do it (p. 168). So, metaphysics can help us to decide what we should do, only if it can show us 'the future consequences of our actions beyond what can be established by ordinary **inductive reasoning**' (p. 168).

69   However, metaphysicians usually hold that metaphysics, as well as telling us 'the effects of our actions', can answer the 'primary ethical question' of what is 'good in itself' (p. 169). But as no 'truth about what is real' is relevant to this question, any attempt to 'base Ethics on Metaphysics' is due to 'confusion' (p. 169).

70   One element in this is the 'ambiguity' in the question, 'What is good?'; it can refer to 'existing things' that are good, or the *'sort* of things' that are, whether 'real or not' (p. 169). Metaphysics appears to be relevant to the first question, 'if it can tell us what is real' (p. 170). But the 'business of Ethics' is complete, when it has established what things 'ought to exist', whether they do or not; something's being real is not 'a reason' for thinking it 'good' (p. 170). Further, the view that we need to know 'reality', in order to know the 'Supreme Good', will lose credibility, once we see that, as what we do cannot affect 'what exists eternally', no **'practical maxim'** can be true, if 'the sole reality is eternal', or 'eternal reality' is the 'sole good' (p. 171).

71   When we encounter a 'metaphysical principle of Ethics',

which states, 'This eternal reality is the Supreme Good', to be relevant to ethics, it must mean that something like it 'would be the Supreme Good'; it must refer to the sort of thing that 'ought to exist in the future', and which we should strive to 'bring about' (pp. 171–2). But its being real has no bearing on the 'ethical question' of whether it is good (p. 172). For ethical 'purposes', the 'metaphysical construction of Reality' would be as helpful if it were of an 'imaginary **Utopia**', as this would still give us material on which to '**exercise the judgment of value**' (p. 172). Metaphysics may suggest 'possible ideals', of which we would not otherwise have thought, and which we may 'see to be good', but their being 'real' would not make them more useful (p. 172).

72 As a 'thing's reality' is not a *necessary condition* of its goodness, we do not need metaphysics even to 'furnish *part*' of ethics, but when metaphysicians say it should be based on metaphysics, they mean as its *'sole* basis' (p. 173). They seem to believe, either that proving something 'supersensibly real' is enough to 'prove it good', or that what is 'real' must also be good, because it has certain 'characters' (p. 173). In the same way that Mill believed 'good' meant 'desired', so that the question of what is good could be answered by 'empirical investigation' of 'what was desired', metaphysicians hold that 'good' means having 'some supersensible property', so ethical questions can be answered by identifying the things that have it (p. 174).

73 One reason they think this is that the most common 'type of proposition' relates to 'objects of experience', and asserts a 'relation between two existing things' (p. 174). 'Ethical truths' are thought not to 'conform to this type', and the 'naturalistic fallacy' is an attempt to 'make out' that they do (pp. 174–5). Clearly, a thing's 'goodness' is not 'a property' we can take hold of, but philosophers argue that this is not

because it is a 'different *kind* of object', but because it '*necessarily* exists together with' a particular thing (p. 175). However, while empiricists hold that goodness accompanies something that exists 'here and now', such as what is desired, metaphysicians, who recognize 'truths which do not mean that anything exists here and now', and see that '"good" is a predicate which neither does nor can exist', conclude that it means being related to something in the '"the real world"': that it is 'transcended or absorbed in reality' (p. 176). So, they, too, 'commit the naturalistic fallacy' (p. 176).

74 We have shown that, whatever may be 'proved to exist', it is a 'distinct' question whether it is 'good' (p. 176). Misconceptions also arise from calling what '*ought to be done*' a 'moral *law*' (p. 177). A so-called 'moral law' is only like a 'natural law' (that says things happen '*in all cases*'), or an ordinary 'law' (that commands that things be done), in being '*universal*': it states that something is 'good in all cases' (p. 176). The '**analogy**' is sometimes taken further, but should not be (p. 177).

75 Kant's mistake is to think '**moral law** to be analogous to natural law' (p. 177). He identifies 'what ought to be' with 'the law', by which a '**Free or Pure Will** *must* act': what it 'ought to do *means* nothing but its own law' (p. 177). There is no 'separate standard' for judging it; what the 'Pure Will' does is good, just 'because it is what is necessarily willed by a Pure Will' (p. 177). That the 'Moral Law' is 'dependent upon Freedom' means that no claim that anything is good can be true, unless 'Reality' is as he says (p. 178). If, '"This ought to be done" *means* "This is willed by a Free Will"', proof that there is no free will would mean that 'nothing ought to be done' (p. 178).

76 Another 'fallacy' of Kant's is to think of the moral law as 'an **Imperative**' (p. 178). This 'common mistake' makes 'moral

obligation' analogous to 'legal obligation', and holds that what 'ought to be' means what is 'commanded', ultimately by a 'real supersensible authority' (p. 178). But what is commanded is only a 'source of moral obligation', if it is good, not because it is commanded (p. 179).

77   The idea of 'ought' meaning 'commanded' brings us to the 'commonest assumption' of contemporary 'Metaphysical Ethics': that ethical questions can be answered by investigating 'the nature of a fundamentally real **Will**' (p. 179). This links up with the view that saying a thing 'is real or true' is saying 'it is known in a certain way': that the difference between an 'ethical' and a 'metaphysical proposition' is that the latter relates 'to Cognition', the former 'to Will' (p. 179). I have already proved that something being 'good' is '*not* identical' with its being 'willed', but I shall examine the 'possible connections' between 'goodness and will', to underline the point that the latter is not relevant to proving 'any ethical conclusion' (pp. 179–80).

78   Since 'Kant's time', 'Cognition, **Volition** and Feeling' have been regarded as 'fundamentally distinct attitudes of the mind towards reality', and ethics has been seen as having a 'relation' to will and feeling that it does not to cognition (pp. 180–1).

79   This could mean that we 'become aware of ethical distinctions' through 'feeling and willing', but this is a purely 'psychological fact' (p. 181). It could also mean that willing a thing is 'the *same*' as thinking it 'good'; and it may be that we 'hardly ever' think something good without having 'a special attitude' of 'will towards it' (p. 181).

80   However, having a particular feeling towards something, or preferring it, does not show 'the thing is good', only that 'you think it so' (p. 182). This 'confusion' seems to account for the view that 'the question' of what is good is 'identical'

with the question of what is preferred (p. 182). It is 'certainly false' that '"to be true" *means* to be thought in a certain way', but this view is a central part of Kant's philosophy, as he held that 'what was unified in a certain manner by the **synthetic activity** of thought was *ipso facto* true' (p. 183). The only possible 'connection' between 'being true' and 'being thought in a certain way' is that the second is a *'criterion'* of the first; and the truth of this could only be established by investigation (p. 183).

81 It is 'natural', but 'false', to think that a thing's being true is the same as its being 'thought of in a certain way' (p. 184). What is often not recognized is that, when we say we perceive a thing, we are not only saying our mind is 'cognitive', but also that what it 'cognises is true' (p. 184). If the thing it supposedly perceives is 'untrue', that alone entitles us to say that the thing is not perceived; and this has nothing to do with any fact about our 'state of mind' (p. 184). To say something is true does not *'only'* mean our 'mind' having 'a certain attitude towards it'; but perception has 'come to be regarded' as if it indicated a certain state of mind 'and nothing more' (pp. 184–5).

82 Enquiry into what is 'willed' cannot be 'identical with the ethical enquiry' into what is 'good' (p. 186). The reason for their being thought identical is that, just as the question of what is true is 'confused with the question' of what is 'thought true' so, too, is that of what is good with that of what is 'thought good' (p. 186). As to know a thing to be true involves cognizing it, 'it is assumed' that, for it 'to *be* true at all is the same thing as for it to be cognised' (p. 187). Similarly, it is thought that the difference between being 'truly good', and 'falsely thought so', lies in the first being 'the object of a volition differing from that of which an apparent good is the object' (p. 187).

83 The most we might be able to say is that 'what is willed in a certain way is always *also* good', making its being 'so willed' a useful '*criterion* of its goodness'; but to 'establish' this, we would need to show many 'instances' of 'the objects' of a 'certain kind of will' being good (p. 187). **(1)** It should be 'as easy' to 'prove' that a thing is good, while **(2)**, as things that are good appear to have no 'common' property, apart from their 'goodness', there probably is 'no criterion of goodness' (p. 188).

84 There is no evidence that 'writers' who base their ethics on 'an investigation of will' see it as just a '*criterion* of goodness' (p. 188). They start with it, indicating that they think that '"goodness" is *identical* with being willed' (p. 189). For example, **Green** writes: '*the* common characteristic of the good is that it satisfies some desire', thus failing to recognize that the question of what is good is '*different*' from that of what is 'willed in a certain way', and committing the 'naturalistic fallacy' (p. 189).

85 This chapter's purpose has been to show that 'investigation of a supposed supersensible reality' has no relevance to the issue of what is 'good in itself', because '"good" denotes an ultimate, analysable predicate' (p. 190). However, meta-physics could be relevant to '*practical* Ethics', if it could show the 'future effects' of actions (p. 190). 'Metaphysical writers' appear not to realize that, if the 'sole reality' is 'eternal', or this is the 'sole good', our actions cannot have 'any real effect' (p. 190). One reason why metaphysics is (wrongly) thought 'relevant to Ethics' is because of the view that 'good' refers to 'some *real* property of things' (p. 191). But it is not the case that 'all propositions assert a relation between existents'; nor is it the case that 'to be good is equivalent to being willed or felt in some particular way' (p. 191).

Chapter V (pp. 192–231)

Ethics in Relation to Conduct

86 Thus far, I have tried to show what the 'adjective "good" – *means*' (p. 192). Unless we are 'clear on this point', our 'ethical reasoning' will be 'fallacious' (p. 192). We have seen that all ethical propositions are 'synthetic': they are all based, ultimately, on a proposition, 'which cannot be logically deduced from any other proposition' (p. 193). The 'fundamental principles' of ethics are 'self-evident': which means they are 'evident or true' by themselves, not that their truth depends on their being 'evident to you or me' (p. 193). If an ethical proposition, such as 'Pleasure is the only good', is untrue, it is 'untrue because it is untrue', and for 'no other reason' (p. 194). However, 'I *declare* it untrue', because this is 'evident to me' (p. 194).

87 I have discussed propositions which state that particular things are 'good', and claimed that the 'untruth' of that of 'Intuitionistic' hedonism, that only pleasure is good, is 'self-evident' (p. 194). I could not '*prove*' this, only point out how it 'contradicts' other apparently true propositions (p. 194). But my prospects of tackling the question 'rightly' are better than those of 'Bentham or Mill or Sidgwick', who did not ask 'the question which they professed to answer' (p. 195). As to the issue of what is 'good in itself', so far I have only established the important 'negative' result that pleasure is '*not* the sole good' (p. 195).

88 Before discussing it, I shall address the issue of what 'ought we to do' (p. 196). This requires 'empirical investigation' of the 'kind of effects' particular actions bring about, as well as 'ethical judgment proper': every 'judgment in practical Ethics' is of the type, this causes 'that good thing' (p. 196).

89 All questions of what 'is right' are about the 'cause of a good result' and, contrary to the views of some moralists, 'identical with "useful"' (p. 196). Saying, 'I am morally bound to perform this action', means the world will be 'better' for its being performed than if 'any possible alternative were taken'; and, when ethics lays down 'duties' for us, it means that acting in the ways prescribed 'will always produce the greatest possible sum of good' (pp. 196–7). Not committing murder is a duty, because it will never 'cause so much good to exist in the Universe as its avoidance' (p. 197).

90 (1) Clearly, the intuitionists, who hold that 'what we ought to do' is, like 'what is *good in itself*', 'intuitively certain', are wrong, because the former, unlike the latter, can be 'confirmed or refuted' by 'investigation of causes and effects' (p. 198).

91 (2) However, ethics cannot furnish 'a list of duties', because this would require information about 'all the events' that a possible action might affect throughout an 'infinite future', the 'value' of the action and all 'these effects', and so on (p. 199). The best to be hoped for is for ethics to show which possible action is likely to 'produce the greatest sum of good' (p. 199). And this is a 'useful' task for 'Ethical philosophers' to perform, as it may lead to an action that is 'better than' the one we would 'otherwise adopt' (pp. 199–200).

92 The most 'Practical Ethics' can do is to tell us which, 'among a few alternatives possible', will, 'on the whole, produce the best result' (p. 201). It may tell us which is 'the best' of the 'alternatives' we are likely to consider, and, as we shall then know that, if we do not choose any of them, what we do 'is unlikely to be as good' as if we had, it may tell us which of the alternatives 'we *can* choose' will be the best choice; and this would suffice for 'practical guidance' (p. 201).

93 (3) But even establishing the 'probability' that 'doing one thing' will produce a 'better total result' than doing

another is immensely difficult (p. 201). Indeed, 'no sufficient reason' has ever been given for thinking 'one action more right or more wrong than another' (pp. 201–2). It would require considering effects through 'an infinite future', but our 'causal knowledge' only enables us to work out the effects of different possible actions over a 'comparatively short space of time' (p. 202). In general, we believe we have 'acted rationally', if we have 'secured a balance of good' over a 'few years or months', although the fact is that we have 'no rational ground' for 'asserting that one of two alternatives is even probably right and another wrong' (pp. 202–3).

94 The most 'Practical Ethics' can hope to do is to provide 'general rules' about which of a 'few alternative actions' will '*generally* produce the greatest balance of good in the immediate future'; and we cannot be certain that even the 'commands' not to lie or murder are '*universally* better than the alternatives' (pp. 203–4). An 'ethical law' can never be more than 'a generalisation': no two actions produce 'precisely the same' effects, and, although those that are 'important for good or evil, may be generally the same', it is most unlikely they 'will always be so' (pp. 204–5).

95 If we limit our search to '*generally* better' actions, we shall probably find that most of the rules, 'universally recognised by Common Sense', are of this type (p. 205). For example, it seems possible to establish that murder is 'generally wrong', given people's strong 'desire to live' and that the 'common practice' of murder would create a sense of 'insecurity' (p. 206). A 'similar defence' could be made for other 'commonly recognised' rules, such as those to do with 'industry, temperance' and 'keeping of promises' (p. 206). **(1)** They all seem to be of the type that are 'good as a means' in any 'known state of society', which values life and property

(p. 207). **(2)** Indeed, 'preservation of civilised society', without which nothing 'held to be good in itself' could exist, appears to depend upon such 'rules' (p. 207).

96   This does not apply to all the rules of '**Common Sense morality**', some of which only seem to have '**utility**' under present social 'conditions' (p. 207). Utilitarians defend rules on, for example, '**Chastity**', which, they say, reflect such feelings as '**conjugal** jealousy', and so aid the 'conservation of society' (p. 208). But, if 'civilised society' could exist without such rules, chastity would have to be defended on other grounds, which would require more rigorous 'examination' of the 'primary ethical question of what is good and bad' than has been undertaken previously (p. 208).

97   'Sanctions', such as 'legal penalties' and 'social disapproval', are also reasons for obeying such rules; and, they are 'justifications', as well as 'motives' (p. 208). As 'punishment' produces a 'greater evil' than 'omission of the action', it is 'an adequate reason for regarding an action as generally wrong' (pp. 208–9).

98   Even rules that are seen as 'universally good as means' only seem to be so in current 'conditions': certain generally 'recognised and practised' rules have a 'definite utility' in preserving our society (p. 209). But much '**moral exhortation**' is devoted to urging obedience to rules that are '*not* generally practised', and for which no case can be 'conclusively made' (p. 209). Indeed, it 'seems doubtful' that ethics can ever 'establish the utility' of any rules, apart from 'generally practised' ones (p. 210). By classifying actions as 'duties', we identify them as ones: **(1)** that '*everybody* ought to perform'; **(2)** which will '*generally* produce better results than the alternative'; **(3)** and which will be 'useful in any state of society that seems possible' (p. 211).

99 What should the individual do in situations **(a)** where a 'general rule' applies, and **(b)** where it does not (p. 211)? In **(a)**, we can say that a *'generally* useful' rule should *'always'* be observed, not because it will always be 'useful', but because there is more 'probability of its being so' than of our being able correctly to decide that it will not (p. 212). Further, even if we did know we were in a situation where it would be beneficial to 'break the rule', the example we would set might lead others to break it when it was 'not advantageous' to do so (p. 212). Thus, it is best *'always* to conform to rules which are both generally useful and generally practised' (p. 213).

100 In **(b)**, once we move away from 'generally practised and strongly sanctioned' rules, there are 'hardly any' for which there are not 'equally good arguments' both 'for and against' (p. 214). Some 'moralists' say we should always behave 'alike', but, in cases of 'doubt', instead of 'following rules' that may not produce 'good effects', we should consider 'the intrinsic value or vileness' of the 'effects' of our actions, and act accordingly: but this area of ethics has been 'uniformly neglected' (p. 215). What is attainable should also be considered: a more attainable, lesser good is 'to be preferred' to a greater, less attainable one (p. 215). Three helpful 'principles' are: **(1)** it is better to aim at a 'lesser' good, for which a person has a 'strong preference', than a 'greater' one, for which he does not; **(2)** it is more realistic to aim at 'goods', in which he has a 'strong personal interest', than 'more extended beneficence'; **(3)** goods, attainable in the near future or 'present', are preferable to those attainable in a 'further future' (pp. 215–16). A good thing that exists now has 'the same value' as the 'same kind' of good thing that may exist 'in the future'; thus, 'certain attainment of a present good' will generally have the 'strongest claims upon us' (p. 216).

101 **(4)** A 'right' or 'duty' is 'a means to good', so the 'common distinction' between these and the **'expedient'** or 'useful' goes (p. 216). Our 'duty' is simply the 'means to the best possible': the only 'fundamental distinction' in ethics is between 'what is good in itself' and 'what is good as a means' (pp. 216–17). So, is there a distinction between 'duty' and 'expediency' (p. 217)? Duties belong to the 'class of actions which excite moral approval'; that individuals are 'tempted to omit'; and non-performance of which has 'disagreeable' consequences for others (p. 217). 'Expedient actions' are ones we are strongly inclined to perform, and which will have good 'effects upon the **agent**' (p. 218). But nothing entitles us 'to infer' that duties are 'more useful' than expedient actions (p. 218). We could only try 'to *prove* an action's expediency', by asking the same question we would of a duty: will it have the 'best possible effects on the whole' (p. 218)? So, the 'distinction' between the two is that the latter requires enforcement 'by sanctions', because of the 'temptation' not to perform it (p. 219).

102 It is not the same with '"interested" actions', where we seem to be talking only of whether the *'effects upon me* are the best possible': what will be best for me will not necessarily 'produce the best possible results on the whole' (p. 219). Although 'my interest' must be 'something truly good', it is only 'one among possible good effects', and thus may produce 'less good on the whole' than acting in another way (p. 219). The main difference between 'duty' and 'interest' does not seem to be this 'possible conflict', but that the latter action has its 'most obvious effects on the agent', and so he is not inclined to 'omit' it (p. 220).

103 **(5) Aristotle** defines a 'virtue' as a 'habitual disposition' to act in certain ways (p. 220). Virtues are 'commonly regarded as good in themselves', which 'partly consists in an attribution to them of intrinsic value' (p. 220). But I do not agree. We apply the same 'test' to a virtue or a duty: is it a 'means to good' (p. 221)? Thus, 'virtue' can be defined as a 'habitual disposition' to carry out actions that usually 'produce the best possible results'; and, generally, these are duties (p. 221). Virtues also require praise, because of the tendency to 'neglect the actions to which they lead' (p. 221). To call something a virtue, we must be able to show that the disposition 'in question' is better 'as a means' than any 'alternatives possible' (p. 222).

104 Only 'intuition' can decide if 'virtues' and 'duties' are 'good in themselves' (p. 222). Some 'moralists' claim 'virtue' as the 'best of goods', and most have thought this to be either 'virtue or pleasure'; but this is due to the question's meaning not being 'clearly apprehended' (p. 222). They do not see that 'intrinsic value' is a 'simple and unique' notion, and have not distinguished what 'ought we to do', because it has intrinsic value, from what ought to be done as a 'means' to it (p. 222). Virtue is a 'means to good', and is no more the 'sole or chief good' than pleasure (p. 222). But virtues, being 'complex mental facts', are more likely to include things that are 'good in themselves' than pleasure (p. 223).

105 **(1)** Most virtues, though 'valuable as means', have no 'intrinsic value', and **(2)** are not the 'sole good' (p. 223). Those who claim virtue is the sole good, have other, 'contradictory' views (p. 223). Christians say virtue is 'rewarded' by something other than itself: **heaven**, which brings 'happiness'; but this is different from virtue (p. 223). Kant's position, that virtue makes us '*worthy* of happiness', contradicts his claim that only a '**Good Will**' has intrinsic value, by suggesting that a state combining virtue and happiness is 'better in itself' than one lacking the latter (pp. 223–4).

106 **(a)** People 'habitually' carry out duties, without thinking whether 'any good will result from them' (p. 224). I 'habitually' refrain from theft, and so 'have the virtue of honesty' (p. 224). But, although it is useful for a virtue to be thus 'habitual or instinctive', it is a 'gross absurdity' (of which 'Aristotle is guilty') to describe a 'disposition to perform' an action, which has merely '"external rightness"', as 'good in itself' (p. 225). Purely **'external rightness'** has no 'intrinsic value', and it is wrong to believe that just calling 'a thing a virtue' means it is present (pp. 225–6).

107 **(b)** A person's character may be such that, when he does 'a particular duty', he feels 'a love of some **intrinsically good** consequence', which he expects to follow from his action (p. 226). Here there is 'something intrinsically good', and, when someone is thus motivated, we call the 'disposition a virtue' (p. 226). Christianity, by stressing the importance of the '"**inward" disposition**', has done ethics 'a service' (p. 226). But we should be aware of two important, but neglected, 'distinctions' (p. 226). The **New Testament** is concerned with promoting such virtues as 'justice' and 'mercy' ('as against mere ritual observances'), which are *'merely* good as means' (p. 227). We must distinguish this aspect of New Testament 'teaching' from its insistence that being 'angry without a cause' is 'as bad' as actually committing murder (p. 227). The New Testament commends some things that are 'good as means', and others that are 'good in themselves', without distinguishing them (p. 227). **Jesus** may be correct to say that an angry man's 'state' is 'as bad' as a murderer's, but the implication that it *'also causes* as much evil' is wrong (p. 227). Christianity 'praises things merely good as means' as if they were 'good in themselves', and vice versa. Also, it is not only Christianity that stresses the intrinsically valuable 'elements in virtues': Plato does so too (p. 227).

108 **(c)** Christianity stresses 'the value of one particular
motive': the feeling, 'excited by the idea' of an action's 'rightness' (p. 227). The 'idea of **abstract "rightness"**', and its associ-
ated emotions, 'constitute' the '**conscience**' (p. 227). A 'conscientious' person has this idea of an action's **internal rightness**,
and acts only on it (p. 228). But Kant is wrong about this being
the '*only* motive' the New Testament treats as 'intrinsically
valuable'; it also teaches the 'value' of 'what Kant terms mere
"natural inclinations", such as pity' (p. 228). The 'emotion
excited by rightness' is intrinsically valuable, but not more so
than love of things 'good in themselves' (p. 228). Although it
is 'generally useful', 'very harmful actions' may result from
'conscientious motives': conscience is not an infallible guide
to 'what actions are right' (p. 229).

109 **(1)** 'Ethical judgments on conduct' pose questions
about what is 'good as a means': about what we ought to do,
not what 'ought to be', and can only be answered by showing
the causal relation of actions to 'what is good in itself' (p. 229).
(2) To call an action a 'duty' is to state that it is a 'possible
action', which, in 'certain known circumstances', will '*always*'
lead to 'better results than any other'; and this requires 'a
proof' that it is beyond our present knowledge to give (p. 230).
(3) All ethics has tried to do is to show that certain actions
'*generally* produce better or worse total results' than likely
alternatives; and this may make it possible to show that, in
'certain conditions of society', the 'commonest rules of duty
are true' (p. 230). People should '*always* perform' actions, the
'*general* utility' of which has been established (p. 230). Where
it has not been, they should use their own judgement about
the likely results of their actions. **(4)** The only difference
between a duty and an 'expedient' or 'interested' action is

that the former has 'certain non-ethical predicates' (p. 230). A
virtue is a 'permanent disposition' to carry out duties (p. 230).
It is good *'as a means'*, but 'generally has no value in itself',
and, where it does, is not the 'sole good' (pp. 230–1).

Chapter VI (pp. 232–73)

The Ideal

110   This title is 'ambiguous' (p. 232). The 'ideal' may be
(1) the *'best* state of things *conceivable'* (the **'Summum Bonum**
or **Absolute Good'**); **(2)** the 'best *possible* state of things in this
world' (the best we could *'possibly* bring about' or 'Utopia');
(3) what is 'good in itself in a high degree' (pp. 232–3). Here,
the 'third sense' of ideal is addressed, by trying to answer the
'fundamental question of Ethics': what things are 'good or
ends in themselves' (p. 233).

111   How does this question relate to the other two? **(1)** The
'Absolute Good' may consist of 'qualities' we cannot 'imagine', so it is *'possible'* we 'cannot discover' it (p. 233). But we
cannot say definitely that what 'we cannot imagine' is better
than 'things which we can', so our 'search for the Ideal' will
be confined to looking for a whole, composed of familiar 'elements', which, though we shall not be able to say that it certainly is 'Perfection', seems *'better'* than the rest (p. 234). Our
'best ideal' will consist of as many things with 'positive value'
as possible, with nothing 'evil or indifferent' in it (p. 234). One
problem is that many accounts of 'an Ideal' omit a lot of things
of 'positive value' (p. 234). They are often limited to 'the *best*
of single things', whereas there are many positive goods, and
any 'whole' containing them all must be 'of vast complexity'

(p. 234). **(2)** In contrast, utopias are often 'constructed on the principle' of omitting 'great positive evils', and including things that are 'mere means to good', and which have 'no value in themselves' (p. 235). To decide what 'we ought to aim' at, we need to consider, not only what is obtainable, but what has 'the greatest value': so the 'comparative valuation of known goods' is as relevant to investigation of utopias as to 'the Absolute Good' (p. 235).

112 To determine what has 'intrinsic value', we must identify what would be judged good, if they 'existed *by themselves*'; and then determine their 'comparative value' (p. 236). This approach will **(1)** eliminate things that are good only as 'means', and **(2)** prevent neglect of the 'principle of organic unities', as it will be clear whether a particular property, which is 'part of a whole' has, or has not, as 'much value' as 'the whole, of which it forms a part' (p. 236).

113 The 'most valuable things' are, undoubtedly, 'the pleasures of human intercourse and the enjoyment of beautiful objects' (p. 237). It is the 'fundamental truth of **Moral Philosophy**' that it is only for their sake, and so they may exist as abundantly as possible, that there is any purpose in 'performing any public or private duty', or being virtuous (p. 238). These 'complex wholes' are 'the rational ultimate end of human action and the sole criterion of social progress' (p. 238). However, that '**personal affections** and **aesthetic enjoyments**' comprise '*all*' and 'the greatest goods we can imagine' tends to be 'generally overlooked' (p. 238).

114 I **(1)** Taking the second first, 'appreciation' of a 'beautiful object' includes both 'bare cognition of what is beautiful' and 'feeling or emotion' (p. 238). The '*beauty*' of the object needs to be felt and seen, and 'the whole', comprising 'consciousness' of a particular 'kind of beauty' and the appropriate

71

'emotion', is 'better' than if another (inappropriate) emotion had been felt (pp. 238–9). However, as the 'wholes are organic', the emotion, *'by itself'*, would not necessarily have 'value', and might be 'positively bad', if applied to something else, such as what is 'ugly' (p. 239).

115 (2) Both the emotion and the 'cognitive element' (it also has little value by itself) must be present to 'form these highly valuable wholes' (p. 239). The latter is 'the actual cognition or consciousness of any or all of an object's *beautiful qualities*': those that possess 'positive beauty' (p. 240). That this is 'essential to a valuable whole' is evident from the fact that little value would attach to 'the proper emotion' aroused by 'Beethoven's Fifth Symphony', if there was no 'consciousness' of either the 'notes', or the 'melodic and harmonic relations between them' (pp. 240–1).

116 (3) It is rightly thought that seeing beauty in something that has it is better than seeing it in something that does not. But the latter could mean one of two things: ascribing to an object 'really beautiful qualities' that it lacks, or having for actual qualities, which are not beautiful, a feeling that would only be 'appropriate', if they were (p. 241). The first is 'an error of judgment', involving 'a false judgment *of fact*', the second, one 'of taste', involving 'a false judgment *of value*' (p. 241). The second has 'no value', apart from that of 'the emotion', and may be a 'positive evil': seeing beauty in a thing lacking it, is 'inferior in value' to seeing it where it actually is (p. 241). The first one is harder, as there is 'cognition' of 'really beautiful' qualities, and an 'appropriate emotion' (pp. 241–2). However, as 'what is believed' in relation to the object 'is false', does this false belief affect the 'value' of the 'whole' (p. 242)?

Where there is 'cognition' of beautiful qualities and 'the appropriate emotion', there may also be: belief in the existence of these qualities, and they exist; 'mere cognition, without belief', when it is '**(a)** true, **(b)** false' that they exist; or belief in the existence of the qualities, 'when they do not exist' (p. 242). The first relates to appreciation of natural beauty and 'human affections'; the second 'defines the pleasures of imagination', including 'appreciation' of works of *'representative'* **art**; the third relates to 'misdirected affection', and may include a believer's 'love of God' (p. 242).

117 With 'purely imaginative appreciations', where there is no belief in the cognized object's existence or non-existence, the issue of existence has no effect on 'the value of the total state' (p. 243). But with the other two, belief in the object's 'reality' makes the 'total state' better, if true, but worse, if it is not (p. 243). And, if this is so, we have 'vindicated' the view that *'knowledge'*, as opposed to 'belief in what is false', or 'mere awareness of what is true', can make 'a whole more valuable' than it would otherwise be (p. 243). Thus, those with a high regard for truth would tend to believe that the poet's 'contemplation of the **Kingdom of Heaven**' is 'superior' to the religious believer's, if the kingdom of heaven does not exist (p. 243).

118 **(a)** With belief, the truth or falsity of its object affects its value *'as a means'*: we are likely to act on our beliefs, so their being true rules out 'disappointment' and other 'serious consequences' (p. 244). Belief in God may make the believer do things that, if he does not exist, are worse than the things he might have done otherwise. The main reason why natural beauty is considered superior to that in a painting or 'imagination' is that this ensures more frequent 'emotional contemplation' of it (p. 244). **(b)** The 'existence' of what we 'contemplate' may be a 'great positive good', and so 'intrinsically superior' to its not existing (pp. 244–5). This is particularly so with 'human affections', which involve admiring a worthwhile person's 'mental qualities': the existence of two 'admirable persons' is better than that of only one (p. 245).

119 But is the 'value' of such a 'whole' greater than that of those where there is either 'absence of belief, with or without truth', or, there being belief, 'absence of truth' (p. 245)? This is not about its superiority 'as a means', or its containing a 'more valuable *part*', the 'existence of the object in question', but whether its existence is 'an addition to the value of the whole, quite distinct from' its being a 'valuable part' (pp. 245–6). I think it is. Imagine someone who spends his life contemplating beautiful 'scenery', and interacting with 'admirable' persons, yet the objects are 'unreal' (p. 246). We would regard such a universe as '*greatly* inferior in value' to one in which the objects existed, '*not only*' because its 'goods' do not actually exist, but '*also*' because this person's 'belief would be false' (p. 246). I can illustrate this point: **(1)** The limited value attached to the existence of 'inanimate objects' does not 'nearly equal' the 'difference' between the value attached to 'appreciation' of ones that actually exist, as opposed to 'imaginative appreciation' of those that do not (p. 246). **(2)** The addition to value 'true belief' makes can also be shown by the case of a person whose 'object of affection' is another who exists, but whose 'qualities' are not 'the *same*' as those 'loved' (p. 247). This is a much less 'satisfactory' situation than one in which the 'very person loved' actually exists (p. 247).

120 'True belief' in an object's reality 'greatly increases the value of many valuable wholes' (p. 247). 'Aesthetic and affectionate emotions' lack value without 'cognition of appropriate objects'; this lacks value without the 'appropriate emotion'; and thus a whole, combining both, has a much greater value than 'the sum of the values of its parts' (p. 247). If true belief in the object's reality is added, the new whole's value greatly exceeds the 'sum obtained' by the addition of the value of the true belief, 'considered in itself', to that of the 'original wholes' (p. 247). **(1)** This section seems to vindicate the great 'intrinsic value' attached to 'mere *knowledge* of some truths', and to show that, though having little value 'by itself', it is an 'essential constituent in the highest goods': knowledge of the 'nature of the constituents of a beautiful object' seems to add to the value of contemplating it (pp. 247–8). **(2)** Even where there is 'great inferiority' in the value of an emotion and the 'beauty of its object', combining true belief with them may create a whole 'equal or superior' in value to those where the former is 'superior', but the latter is lacking (p. 248). God may be 'more perfect' than any human being, but 'love of God' may be 'inferior to human love, *if* God does not exist' (p. 248).

121 **(4)** Full discussion of 'goods' relating to '*beautiful* objects' would require 'classification' and 'valuation' of the 'different forms of beauty', which I shall not attempt; I believe there is enough 'consensus' about what is 'beautiful' and 'ugly' to prevent errors in 'judgments' (pp. 248–9). However, two important points should be kept in mind. **(1)** The naturalistic fallacy occurs as often in relation to beauty as to good, with the claim that 'beautiful' can be '*defined*' subjectively, as that which 'produces certain effects upon our feelings' (p. 249). In fact, whether or not a thing is beautiful is determined by the '*objective*' issue of whether or not it is 'truly good', which also explains the 'connection between goodness and beauty' (pp. 249–50). 'Good' is the only '*unanalysable* predicate of value', but 'beautiful', though not 'identical with' it, is 'to be defined by reference to' it; proving something beautiful means that the whole, of which it is part, is 'truly good' (p. 250). **(2)** Beautiful things are mainly complex 'organic unities'; there is no value in contemplating a part alone, or the whole

without it (p. 250). There is no 'single criterion of beauty', such that beautiful objects always have one or more common 'characteristics' (pp. 250–1). The 'specific qualities' that make one beautiful object different from others are as *'essential* to its beauty' as any **generic qualities**' it shares with them (p. 251).

122 II With 'personal affection', the object itself is 'of great intrinsic value', and must be both 'truly beautiful' and 'truly good in a high degree' (p. 251). A 'large part' of the 'most valuable' affection concerns 'mental qualities', but 'appreciation' of their 'appropriate *corporeal* expression' will make it more so; it is hard to think what 'cognition of mental qualities *alone*' would be (pp. 251–2). The 'most valuable appreciation of a person' seems to be of their 'attitude' towards others: 'love of love' is a far more 'valuable good' than mere 'love of beauty', but only seems to be so, if it includes 'the latter' (pp. 252–3). As to the nature of the 'mental qualities' that have to be cognized, to make 'human intercourse' valuable, they include the various emotions, 'appropriate to persons', as well as to 'mere corporeal beauty' (p. 253). This matter is of 'immense complexity', containing much that is of 'no value', or 'positively bad' (p. 253). But 'reflective judgment' should be able to determine the 'positive goods', while the emotions that must be contemplated for the 'greatest values' seem to be those generally 'prized under the name of affection' (p. 253).

123 This completes my enquiry into 'great positive goods' that do not contain anything 'positively evil or ugly' (p. 254). What can we now say about the 'Summum Bonum' (p. 254)? Many philosophers, who accept pleasure is not 'the sole good', and that the good is complex, regard it as a 'purely spiritual state of existence' and matter as 'imperfect', if not 'evil' (p. 254). Now, the spiritual's 'superiority' over 'the material' has been shown, but this does not mean that a 'perfect state'

76

is one without 'material properties' (p. 254). We must bear in mind the maxim: that 'everything is what it is, and not another thing' (p. 254). What we value are 'organic' unities, which include *'cognition of material qualities'* that seem to be 'essential constituents' of valuable things (pp. 254–5). If we remove them, we are left with 'something else', so it looks as if they are a 'necessary' part of 'the Ideal' (p. 255). A *'purely* spiritual good' may be the *'best* of single things', but 'adding to it' some 'appreciation of material qualities' seems to give 'a greater sum of value' (p. 256).

124 There are two further 'topics', relating to the 'determination of intrinsic values': the 'nature of great intrinsic *evils*', which includes *'mixed* **evils**'; and *'mixed* **goods**' (good wholes that contain 'evil or ugly' elements) (p. 256). I 'Great positive evils' (things that, *'if they existed absolutely by themselves'*, we would consider a 'great evil') are, like the 'greatest positive goods', 'organic unities': 'cognition' of an object, together with 'an emotion' (p. 256). Neither of these, *'by itself'*, seems 'capable of being greatly evil', but a whole, 'formed of both', does (pp. 256–7). As for *'true belief'*, it seems to have 'different relations towards different kinds of evils' (p. 257). There are 'three classes' of 'positive evils' (p. 257).

125 **(1)** The first involves 'admiring contemplation' of the 'evil or ugly' (p. 257). As the emotion itself has some beauty, we seem to be dealing with 'mixed' evils, but it is hard to attach value to an emotion that is 'completely isolated' from its proper object (p. 257). It is important to note, though, that the 'same emotions' may be 'conditions' of either the 'greatest good' or the 'greatest evil' (p. 257). Let us take 'cruelty and **lasciviousness**' (p. 257). A mental universe, dominated by such 'passions', would be worse than 'none at all'; they are 'bad' as 'means' and 'in themselves' (pp. 257–8). Both involve 'love of what is evil': the second, enjoyment of the same 'state of mind' in others; the first, pleasure in others' pain; and, the 'intrinsic odiousness' of cruelty is the same, whether the pain is real or 'imaginary' (pp. 258–9). Indeed, *'true belief'* in their objects' existence has no bearing on the 'demerits' of evils of this sort (p. 259). Further, enjoying what we know to be 'evil or ugly' increases the 'intrinsic vileness of our condition' (p. 259).

126 (2) While the first class of evils involves directing an emotion, 'appropriate to the cognition of what is good', to an 'inappropriate object' (loving the 'evil or ugly'), 'mixed evils' concern 'cognition of what is good', combined with an 'inappropriate emotion' (hating the 'good or beautiful') (pp. 259–60). Such 'vices' as 'hatred' and 'envy' are examples, and evils of the 'first class' often accompany them, making them worse, as when someone takes pleasure in a good person's 'pain' (p. 260). They are also made worse by 'true belief' in the existence of the hated 'good or beautiful object', and in the *'value* of the objects contemplated' (p. 260).

127 (3) Pains constitute the 'third class of positive evils' (p. 260). As with pleasure, our concern is with 'consciousness' of it: pain (however great), of which there was no consciousness, would not be an evil (p. 260). The difference is that, whereas pleasure is not a *'great* good', *'by itself'*, 'mere cognition' of pain, on its own, is a 'great evil' (pp. 260–1). Further, while pleasure seems to 'enhance the value of a whole' in which it is joined with another 'great unmixed' good, such that *'only* wholes' that contain a degree of pleasure have 'any great value', pain, though a great evil itself, does not add to the 'badness of a whole' in which it is joined with something else that is bad, apart from 'that which consists in its own intrinsic badness' (p. 261).

128 But they are alike in the following respect: neither

pleasure, nor pain necessarily makes a 'state of things' respectively better or worse, *'on the whole'*, than they would otherwise be (p. 262). Thus, if pleasure is added to an evil state of affairs, the resulting whole is *'always'* worse, as in an evildoer's 'delight' in his 'successful hatred' (p. 262). Similarly, causing pain to someone with a bad 'state of mind' may create a better state of affairs *'on the whole'* than if it had gone 'unpunished', but it is debatable whether this could produce 'a *positive* good' (p. 262).

129 II Mixed goods are things which, 'though positively good *as wholes*', include, as 'essential elements', things that are 'intrinsically evil' (p. 262). To say they are 'positively good *as wholes*', means they are 'positively good *on the whole*': a thing's value *'on the whole'* is its sum of value *'as a whole, together with* the intrinsic values which may belong to any of its parts' (p. 263).

130 (1) Can such wholes as '**retributive punishment**', which comprises two 'great positive evils' ('wickedness and pain'), be 'positively good *on the whole*' (p. 264)? There is 'no reason' to think so, but, as these wholes may be lesser 'evils' than 'either of their parts' alone, this highlights an important point when it comes to deciding 'practical questions' (p. 264). If an evil 'already exists', it may be worthwhile creating another, as this may produce 'a whole less bad' than if the original evil had been allowed to 'exist by itself' (p. 264).

131 (2) Wholes, 'containing something positively evil', may be 'great positive goods on the whole' (p. 265). Virtues, like 'courage and compassion', seem to require 'cognition of something evil', and *'hatred'* of it, and are examples of 'mixed goods' (p. 265). Pity for others' 'undeserved' suffering, and 'endurance' of our own pain, seem 'admirable in themselves', and would not exist without 'cognition of evil' (pp. 265–6).

I cannot distinguish the '"moral" sentiment', as it relates to the ideas of right and wrong, from a 'state' of cognizing 'something intrinsically evil', and having an 'emotion of hatred' for it (p. 266). This is not surprising: many duties are *negative*, involving our refraining from actions we are tempted to do (p. 266). To act rightly is often to suppress an 'evil impulse', and the 'intrinsic value' of the 'specific moral emotion' is due to its involving 'cognition of evils', together with 'hatred of them' (pp. 266–7).

132 With many virtues, the value of a 'great good' depends on the presence of 'something evil' (p. 267). Although only 'feeling contemplation' of an object that would be a 'great evil', if it existed, is essential to 'a valuable whole' (compassion may be felt for 'imaginary' sufferings), 'conscious compassion' for 'real suffering' seems better, *as a whole*, despite the fact that the evil of actual suffering makes the total situation 'bad *on the whole*' (p. 267).

133 There are three points about 'mixed goods'. **(1)** While the 'appropriate mental attitude' towards a 'real existing evil' is a 'positive good', the quantity of the former will always bring the 'total sum of value' down to a 'negative quantity' (p. 268). This rules out the 'paradox' that, in an 'ideal world', actual 'suffering' and 'wickedness' must exist, so we can feel compassion or hatred for them (p. 268). We must reject the arguments we find in '**Theodicies**': there is no justification even for 'the smallest' of the world's 'many evils' (p. 268). **(2)** Cognition of 'purely imaginary' evils seems necessary to 'the Ideal'; such virtues as compassion and courage include positive goods that require 'cognition of things which would be evil, if they existed' (p. 269). There is no reason to think that 'any whole' lacking them would be as good, *on the whole*, as one containing them, and the argument for 'the Ideal' including them is as powerful as that for its containing 'material qualities' (p. 269). **(3)** From a practical viewpoint, where evils already exist, as in 'this world', it has 'greater value *as a whole*', for them to be 'pitied or hated', according to their 'nature', rather than as 'imaginary evils', even though this is 'never positively good *on the whole*' (p. 269).

134 Many judgements in this chapter may seem 'arbitrary' and lacking in 'symmetry and system', but there is no reason to expect the latter in ethics; I am satisfied that mine is the right approach to the 'fundamental' ethical question (pp. 270–1). 'Many and various' things are 'intrinsically good or bad', and most are 'organic unities' (p. 271). The only way to decide their 'intrinsic value' is to identify them clearly, and see if they have the 'unique predicate "good"' (p. 271). I have tried to avoid the common errors of ethics, and (which is 'entirely new') to ask of the 'objects of ethical judgment': 'Has it intrinsic value?' and 'Is it a means to the best possible?' (pp. 271–2).

135 The main purpose of this chapter has been to identify the 'class of things' that are 'great intrinsic goods' or 'evils', and to show their great 'variety' and that they are 'complex wholes' (p. 272). They involve 'consciousness of', and an 'emotional attitude' towards, an object, but the ways they differ are numerous and 'equally essential to their value', while neither their common, nor their specific, characteristics are 'greatly good' or 'evil' by themselves (p. 272). **(1)** 'Unmixed goods' are 'love of beautiful things' or 'good persons', but there are many 'different goods' of this type (p. 272). **(2)** 'Great evils' comprise **(a)** love of the 'evil or ugly', **(b)** hatred of the 'good or beautiful', and **(c)** 'consciousness of pain' (p. 273). **(3)** 'Mixed goods' have an 'evil or ugly' element: either hatred of evils or 'compassion for pain' (p. 273).

Overview

The following section is a chapter-by-chapter overview of the
six chapters in Moore's *Principia Ethica*, designed for quick
reference to the Detailed Summary above. Readers may also
find this section helpful for revision.

Preface to The First Edition (pp. 33–7)

Moore explains that *Principia Ethica* will try to answer the
two major ethical questions of determining what things
have intrinsic value, and which actions are right. He believes
there is no evidence relevant to the first question, while many
different considerations make it hard to answer the second.

Chapter I   The Subject Matter of Ethics (pp. 53–88)

1 Whenever we say something is good, or we ought to
perform an action, we are making ethical judgements, but
different moral philosophers have given very different answers as to what is common and peculiar to these. 2 Some
think ethics is just about good or bad human conduct, but
other things are good, so it refers to a common property they
and conduct have. He will examine what is good and bad in
general. 3 Many answers to questions about what is good are
not part of ethics. 4 Casuistry covers the same sort of area
as ethics, but tries to discover which actions are right in every
possible situation, but this is an ultimate, not a currently
achievable, goal in ethics. 5 The fundamental question of
ethics is how to define 'good': ethical enquiry is futile, unless
it is understood, and answered. 6 This question concerns
the object the word generally stands for, which cannot be

defined. **7** Like yellow, 'good' is a simple notion, which, unlike, for example, a horse, cannot be defined, as it is not a complex object, consisting of many different properties. **8** A horse can be thought of as its constituent parts, rather than as a whole, but nothing could be substituted, in the same way, for 'good'. **9** But 'the good', the substantive, as opposed to the adjective, is definable.

10 'Good' is one of many objects of thought that cannot be defined, because they are ultimate terms of reference. It may be that all good things are also something else, and the job of ethics is to identify these properties. But many philosophers claim to have defined 'good', if they have listed these properties, which they say are the same as goodness. This is the naturalistic fallacy. **11** They do not agree about the properties, which include, for example, pleasure and what is desired: but, if good is just defined as a particular property, no other definition can be proved wrong. **12** If someone tried to define pleasure as another natural object, such as red, he would be ridiculed, but this is the same as committing the naturalistic fallacy. Pleasure is indefinable, but this does not make it hard to know we are pleased, or to say it is good; but pleasure does not mean 'good', or vice versa. There is no reason to call the fallacy of confusing two natural objects 'naturalistic', but there is when good, which is not a natural object, is confused with something that is, as it happens so often. It does not follow from good's being indefinable that pleasure cannot be good: indeed, unless good and pleasure are different, saying pleasure is good would not mean anything.

13 If 'good' does not denote something simple and indefinable, either it is a complex whole, about correct analysis of which there is disagreement, or it means nothing. The first must be wrong, because, however 'good' is defined, it can always be meaningfully asked, of the complex so defined, whether it is good. 'Good' has often been defined as 'what we desire to desire', but asking whether it is good to desire to desire something is just as intelligible as asking if something is good. It is easy (but wrong) to think that, because things, called 'good', are also pleasant, the proposition, 'pleasure is good', refers to only one concept: pleasure. To say something has intrinsic worth, is to have in mind the unique object, designated by the word 'good'.

14 Sidgwick criticizes Bentham who, as well as saying human action should aim at the greatest happiness of all those whose interest is involved, also seems to say 'right' means 'conducive to general happiness'. This seems to involve a naturalistic fallacy: if 'right' is defined in this way, general happiness is obviously the right end. The greatest happiness may be the proper end of human action, but committing the naturalistic fallacy weakens Bentham's case. To start with the view that 'good' means one particular natural property limits ethical enquiry to discovering it, and will probably cause opposing arguments to be misunderstood, as the question of what is good will not be seen as an open one.

15 Ethical terms refer to the unique notion, 'good' in two ways: by saying a thing is good in itself, or that it is good as a means, that it causes things that are good in themselves. Difficulties arise from not distinguishing them. 16 Saying a thing is good as a cause is to say it has an effect that is good in itself, but universally true causal judgements are rare. We would need to know a certain kind of action always had a particular effect, when the best we can hope for is a generalization that such an effect usually follows it. For the most part, we have to be satisfied with ethical judgements as to what is likely to produce the greatest possible balance of good over

a limited period, and we should bear in mind that common rules of conduct do take account of balancing possible long-term ill effects against immediate gains. We can never be sure of achieving the greatest possible total of good, but must try to prevent likely future ill effects.

17 While judgements that certain kinds of things always have good effects are unlikely to be true, judgements that things are good in themselves will, if true, be universally so. These two kinds of judgements, how far things are good in themselves, and how likely they are to produce good results, are the only questions ethics has to settle. They must be clearly distinguished, but are confused, because ethical questions are often expressed ambiguously. Not everything is achievable, and, when trying to decide what we ought to do, we need to know, not only how much intrinsic value things have, but also how they can be achieved: practical ethical questions always involve this double knowledge.

18 There are things with intrinsic value, positively bad things, and apparently indifferent things, any one of which may be part of a whole that includes things from the same and the other two groups. The paradox is that a whole's value must not be assumed to be the same as the sum of its parts. Consciousness of a beautiful object, consisting of the object and consciousness of it, has great intrinsic value, but a beautiful object seems to have little value, if no one is conscious of it; while, if the object is not beautiful, the consciousness is not valuable either. This is an example of a whole that has a different intrinsic value from the sum of that of its parts.

19 Existence of any such part is a necessary condition of the good of the whole, but the same language is also used to express the relation between the good thing and a means to it. The important difference is that, while the part is a part

of the good thing, and its existence a necessary condition of it, the necessity of any means to it is just causal. However, by itself, the part may have no more intrinsic value than the means, and, although existence of the whole, which includes existence of the part, has intrinsic value, the inference that the part also does would be wrong. **20** As this peculiar relation between part and whole lacks a name, Moore decides to call it 'organic unity'.

21 The parts of the human body form an organic unity, as they have a mutual causal dependence on one another, but neither of two mutually dependent things may have intrinsic value, or only one may. Further, the whole includes all its parts, while no part can be a cause of the whole, as it cannot be a cause of itself. Again, the relation of part and whole is not the same as that between part and part, as when we say that one could not exist without the other. Unlike the latter, the former cannot be causally connected, while their relation may exist, even if the parts are not causally connected, as in the parts of a picture. To say a whole is organic, due to its parts being (in this sense) means to it, is not to say it is organic because its parts are causally dependent on one another.

22 A common misuse of the term 'organic whole' is to indicate that the whole is a part of its parts. Part is not related to whole as whole to part, and it is false to hold that a part has no significance apart from its whole. It is easy to see how this idea has arisen. The existence of a part may be causally connected with other parts of its whole and, when no longer part of it, may have the same name. A dead arm, though not the same thing as a living one, is still called an arm, and so people may say the living one would not be what it is, unless it were part of a whole. But the dead arm was never part of the body, and so is only partially identical with the living one. It is not that properties of the living arm, which the dead one lacks, exist in it in changed form; they do not exist there at all. A different fallacy is saying that, without its body, a living arm lacks significance; but the living arm's value does not belong to it. To be valuable as a part is to have no value, only to be part of something that does. This relation of organic whole to parts is important in ethics, which is concerned with comparing the relative values of various goods. Serious errors arise if it is thought that a whole's value is just the sum of the values of its parts.

23 This section summarizes the contents of the chapter.

Chapter II   Naturalistic Ethics (pp. 89–110)

24 Ethics concerns: what is meant by good; what things are good in themselves; and how to make what exists in the world as good as possible. A number of ethical theories commit the naturalistic fallacy. **25** These fall into two groups: those that define 'good' by reference to a natural object and metaphysical theories. The former divide into those that maintain that pleasure is the sole good and the rest (the subject of Chapter II).

26 These ethical theories claim 'good' means having a natural property, other than pleasure, and so are naturalistic; and 'nature' means the subject-matter of the natural sciences and psychology. The test of natural objects and their properties is existence in time; although good is a property of natural objects, it is not a natural one that could exist by itself in time.

27 One ethical theory is that people should live naturally, suggesting some natural good, fixed by nature, which could be interpreted as something's normal state. But with geniuses, the abnormal is often better than the normal, so whether the normal is good is an open question. 'Good' does not, by definition, mean anything natural, and it is always an open question whether what is natural is good.

28 'Natural' is also used to suggest something good, as in natural affections, as opposed to unnatural crimes. This suggests we cannot improve on nature, and is another example of the naturalistic fallacy. When we say we should do what we think nature prefers, we are taking this to be the highest good, but nature cannot decide what the highest good is.

29 It is a fallacy to claim that something is good or bad, because it is, or is not, natural. Spencer's claim that evolution shows us how we ought to develop is an example of this fallacy. **30** It comes from Darwin's theory of natural selection (that the animal species that became established were ones whose characteristics enabled them to survive in their environment), which suggests (especially with the evolution of human beings) movement from lower to higher. But, Darwin's theory is biological, arguing only that the fittest survives, not the fittest to fulfil a good purpose.

31 Spencer says ethics concerns universal conduct, during the last stages of its evolution, when it becomes more co-operative. He commits the naturalistic fallacy of thinking that 'better' means 'more evolved'. He does not see that any proposition that the former is also the latter needs to be proved.

32 Inconsistently, he also puts forward a different view: that the above would be false, unless life is mainly pleasant. This makes him a hedonist, not an evolutionist: our degree of evolution is only a criterion of ethical value, and can only be that, if the more evolved is always, on the whole, the pleasanter. **33** He argues that everybody's ultimate moral aim is a desirable state of feeling: happiness. This suggests pleasure is the only intrinsically desirable thing; other things

are good only as a means to it; and that more evolved conduct is better as providing more pleasure. But he then says
something else is needed to prove it better: that it should
produce more life. But producing more life is only one way of
providing more pleasure; a small amount of life might yield
more pleasure, making the less evolved conduct preferable for
the hedonist. Spencer seems to want to be both evolutionist
and hedonist. He also claims it causes absurdities, if the word
'good' is used of conduct that produces a balance of pain,
indicating the naturalistic fallacy: that he believes 'pleasant'
is what 'good' means.

34 The term, 'evolutionistic ethics' should be confined to
the fallacious view that the direction of evolution shows us the
way we ought to go. In fact, there is no evidence for believing
that nature is always on the side of what is good.

35 This section summarizes the contents of the chapter.

Chapter III   Hedonism (pp. 111–60)

36 Due to the naturalistic fallacy, that pleasure seems to be
involved in the word's definition, the most widely held ethical principle is that only pleasure is good. Of all hedonistic
writers, only Sidgwick realizes that 'good' means something
unanalysable, and that the belief that pleasure is the only
good is an intuition. **37** Hedonism is a form of naturalism,
and the view that only pleasure is good as an end, or in itself,
is wrong. **38** Hedonists think that everything, other than
pleasure, is good only as means to pleasure, a view held by
utilitarians, like Bentham and Mill. Discussion of its confusions underlines the importance of avoiding the naturalistic
fallacy, and clearly distinguishing means and ends.

39 Mill's *Utilitarianism* deals fairly with many ethical principles, but contains errors in relation to the hedonistic principle. He says that pleasure and freedom from pain are the only things desirable as ends and, having defined 'happiness' as 'pleasure' and 'absence of pain', maintains that it is desirable, and the only thing desirable as an end, while other things are only desirable as means to it. Therefore, Mill uses 'desirable' or 'desirable as an end' as equivalent to the words 'good as an end'. He also says that questions of ultimate ends are not capable of direct proof, and that questions about ends are questions about what things are desirable.

40 Mill's reasons for holding that pleasure alone is good as an end are not convincing. He argues that, just as the only proof that a thing is visible is that people actually see it, the only evidence that anything is desirable is that people actually desire it. The only reason why general happiness is desirable is that each person desires his own happiness. This is all the proof needed that happiness is a good; that each person's happiness is a good to him; and that general happiness is a good to the aggregate of all persons. This is a naïve use of the naturalistic fallacy, for 'desirable' does not mean 'able to be desired', but 'what ought to be desired'. Once this is understood, it is impossible to argue that the only test of it is what is actually desired.

41 Mill has wrongly tried to establish the identity of good by confusing the proper meaning of 'desirable' with what it would mean, if it meant the same as 'visible'. Having established (he believes) that good means desired, to show (as he wishes) that pleasure alone is good, he must prove that only it is really desired. **42** But people desire other things, apart from pleasure, such as money. To justify hedonism, there must be a necessary relation between desire and pleasure. There is, but not one that supports hedonism. While Mill holds that the idea of a pleasure, not actual, is always necessary to cause desire, in fact, an actual pleasure, caused by the idea of (having) something else, is always necessary to cause desire. Mill's psychological hedonism confuses a pleasant thought with the thought of a pleasure; only when there is the latter can pleasure can be said to be the object of desire. When there is only a pleasant thought, it is object of the thought that is the object of desire. Accepting that pleasure is always the cause of desire means rejecting the view that only pleasure is good; pleasure is not what a person desires, but something he must have before he can want anything. **43** Mill has another argument for happiness being the sole end of human action. He acknowledges that people desire things other than pleasure, such as virtue and money, but tries to get round this by saying that, when such things are desired in and for themselves, this is only as a part of happiness. However, he also says they are only desirable as a means to happiness. But, if they are only desirable as a means, how can they also be desirable as ends in themselves? Mill's answer is that what is only a means to an end is the same thing as a part of that end. Thus, Mill has had to eliminate the distinction between means and ends, due to failure to distinguish 'end', in the sense of what is desirable, from 'end', in the sense of what is desired. **44** Mill's basic position is that considering an object desirable and pleasant are the same, and it is completely impossible to desire a thing, except in proportion to the idea of it being pleasant. The first one is based on the naturalistic fallacy, the second on a confusion of ends and means, and of a pleasant thought with the thought of pleasure. For Mill, the desirable means what can be desired, the test of this being what actually is desired. If there is something that is always, and the only thing, desired, that will necessarily be the only desirable thing, and the only thing good as an end. His use of the naturalistic fallacy is obvious. He takes 'good' to mean 'what is desired' but, if 'ought to desire' means 'do desire', he can only say that we desire something, because we desire it. This is a tautology, not an ethical proposition.

45 While Mill's naturalistic arguments for hedonism can be refuted, the proposition that pleasure alone is desirable may still be true. The proposition is a first principle, which cannot be proved directly, but there are considerations that can legitimately incline the mind to accept or reject it. This makes ethical hedonism's basic proposition an object of intuition, but one Moore rejects. By exploring its implications, he hopes to secure agreement that it is absurd. **46** Discussion of intuitionistic hedonism will involve a change in method, as the issue is one where no more than indirect proof is possible. The intuition to be explored is: 'pleasure alone is good as an end'.

47 Moore explains that Bentham bases his argument for hedonism solely on quantity of pleasure, but Mill regards quality as a different ground for estimating pleasures: the more desirable of two pleasures is the one experts prefer, because it is superior in quality. But Mill's view that pleasures differ qualitatively is either inconsistent with his hedonism, or offers no other basis for it than quantity. If a thing's being desirable and pleasant are the same, expert preference can only prove one pleasure pleasanter than another, which would be just the criterion of quantity. But, if there is a qualitative difference, the basis of Mill's hedonism collapses, as he accepts a thing may be more desirable, though not more desired. This appears to make Mill's preference an intuition, and to be an admission that good is good and indefinable.

48 A further implication of the view that pleasures differ qualitatively is that they must be complex, consisting of pleasure and what produces it. Introducing quality of pleasure rules out the claim that pleasure alone is good as an end. There must be something, not present in all pleasures, which is also good as an end, and this is incompatible with the hedonistic principle.

49 Moore points out that Sidgwick rejects Mill's quality test, and relies solely on the hedonistic principle, but he rejects his arguments. **50** Sidgwick argues that the only things commonly judged good relate to human existence or consciousness; but if there could be one of two worlds, a beautiful and an ugly one, neither of which human beings could ever see, it would not be irrational to prefer the beautiful one. This undermines Sidgwick's point, by showing that something is better in itself, independently of its effects on human feeling. So, the ultimate end includes something beyond the limits of human existence. **51** Sidgwick maintains that intuitive judgement and ordinary common-sense judgements indicate that such things as contemplation of beauty are not intrinsically valuable, unless related to conscious existence. They are important because they promote happiness, and are approved to the degree they do so.

52 Moore asks if pleasure is valuable in itself, or only when human beings are conscious of it, as a person could lead a life of intense pleasure, while lacking intelligence, memory or knowledge. Pleasure seems comparatively valueless without consciousness of it, so cannot be the only end: some consciousness must be included with it as part of the end. **53** It cannot be true that only pleasure is desirable, and also that consciousness of it is more desirable still. The latter clearly is true, so pleasure is not the sole good. But not even consciousness of pleasure is the sole good. The same method that shows the latter to be more valuable than pleasure also shows it is less valuable than other things.

54 Sidgwick says our ordinary common-sense judgements about things that might be thought to share the property of goodness with pleasure are related to the degree to which they produce pleasure, but this only shows that pleasure is a good criterion of a right action: that conduct that produces most pleasure also generally produces most good. This does not prove that the greatest pleasure constitutes what is best on the whole, as it leaves open the alternative that the greatest quantity of pleasure is generally accompanied by the greatest quantity of other goods. What Sidgwick tends to show is that something is not held to be good, unless it gives a balance of pleasure, not that approval of it is in proportion to the quantity of pleasure.

55 Sidgwick claims that regarding happiness as only part of what is ultimately good does not fit in with the facts of intuition, but the fact that enjoyment of beauty is valuable, while just contemplating it is not, does not mean that all the value is in the pleasure. It does not follow that, because there is no value in one part of a whole, by itself, all the value is in the other part: both may be equally necessary parts of the good. Sidgwick ignores the principle of organic relations, and holds that, if a whole is valuable, but one part has no value by itself, all the value must be in the other part. But, if the whole is organic, the other part may also be valueless by itself. Sidgwick does not ask if pleasure, by itself, would have much value. As pleasure seems a necessary element in most valuable wholes, it is easy to think that, if the other elements lack value by themselves, all the value lies in it.

56 Sidgwick holds that, in common-sense judgements, things are approved to the degree they promote pleasure, but this could only possibly be true when things are viewed as a means. When judging thing as ends, people often prefer less pleasant to more pleasant states, agreeing with Mill that there are higher and more valuable pleasures. **57** What are desirable are complicated states of mind, combining consciousness of pleasure with other things. The principle of organic unities makes it possible to see that consciousness of pleasure is not the sole good, and that other states, of which it is part, are better.

58 Egoism is a form of hedonism that holds that each should pursue his own greatest happiness as his ultimate end, but the term can denote the view that aiming at one's own pleasure is the best means to increase the general sum of happiness. **59** When a thing is said to be good for someone, this must be the thing itself, not its goodness, which cannot belong to just one person. The only reason for someone pursuing his own good is that it is good absolutely for him to have a thing. If his interest or happiness is his sole ultimate end, it must be the universal good, and so the only thing anyone ought to aim at. Egoism holds that each person's happiness is the sole good, making more than one thing the sole good thing, which is contradictory.

60 Sidgwick says egoism is rational, but something cannot be an ultimate rational end for one person and not another. A thing that is an ultimate rational end must be truly good in itself. Either the egoist's happiness is good in itself, and part of universal good, or it is not good in itself: but there would be no point in the egoist aiming at it, if it were not. Talk of an ultimate rational end for the individual is a contradiction in terms. Egoism leads to the fundamental contradiction that many things are each the sole good. If one person's happiness is desirable, it is part of the universal good, and thus everyone has equal reason to pursue it. Adding 'for him' to 'ultimate rational end' and 'good' causes confusion. An action's only possible justification is to obtain the greatest possible amount of what is good absolutely. When someone claims pursuit of his own happiness justifies his actions, this can only mean this is how he can achieve the greatest possible amount of universal good.

61 Sidgwick considers how pursuit of individual happiness as an end, and the utilitarian duty to promote general happiness, can be reconciled, suggesting belief in God would ensure the latter. His error is thinking that changing facts can remove a contradiction. Egoism's principle, that each individual's happiness should be the sole good, is a contradiction, and universalistic hedonism's principle, that the happiness of all is the sole good, would just create another one. When as much good as possible exists in one place, we secure less on the whole, as the quantity of good attainable is limited. Posing a choice between individual good and that of all creates a false antithesis. The choice is between individual good and that of others.

62 Egoism's self-contradiction is present in the transition from naturalistic hedonism to utilitarianism. Mill thinks he can infer that the 'happiness of all is the good of all' from 'each man's happiness is his own good'. A correct understanding of 'his own good' shows the former can only be inferred from 'the happiness of all is the good of each'. **63** Moore notes that the type of egoism he has just discussed is sometimes thought reasonable, through being confused with egoism as a doctrine of means: sometimes we ought to do what is good only as a means, which could be pursuing our own happiness.

64 The name 'utilitarianism' was adopted to indicate that conduct must be judged by results, and should promote everyone's interest. The view then developed that actions should be judged by the extent to which they are a means to pleasure. Utilitarians tend to think of everything as a means, overlooking the fact that what are good as means are also good as ends. They see current pleasures as means to future ones, judging them by their results, rather than valuing them in themselves. They talk of the greatest happiness of the greatest number but, if pleasure is the sole good, given an equally great quantity of it, the number enjoying it should not matter. If the utilitarian principle means many people having pleasure is good in itself, it is not the hedonistic principle, and includes more than mere pleasure as a necessary part of the ultimate end. In its favour is the fact that acting in ways that bring most good generally brings most pleasure. But, as many complex states of mind are more valuable than the pleasure they contain, Moore concludes that no form of hedonism is true.

65 This section summarizes the contents of the chapter.

Chapter IV   Metaphysical Ethics (pp. 161–91)

66 Metaphysicians hold that ethical truths follow from metaphysical ones. They recognize that not all objects are natural ones, and that some do not exist in time: the class to which what is meant by the adjective 'good' belongs. But they maintain that what does not exist in time must exist in a supersensible reality. **67** They claim that the perfectly good exists, but is not natural. Unlike naturalism, their ethical principles recognize that more is needed for perfect goodness than what exists here and now, but they also claim that what is (metaphysically) real is relevant to what is good. But this commits the naturalistic fallacy, because ethical propositions cannot be inferred from ones about reality. **68** The nature of supersensible reality could be relevant to questions of what we ought to do: for example, if we knew we were immortal. But many metaphysical doctrines concern an eternal reality, which human action could not affect. To be worth making, our efforts must be capable of producing something good, so propositions about what we ought to do could only be consistent with an eternal reality, if it were not the only one.

69 Metaphysicians also claim to be able to answer the primary ethical question of what is good in itself but, as no truth about what is real is relevant to this question, any attempt to base ethics on metaphysics results from confusion. **70** Questions about what is good can refer to existing things that are good, or the kind of things that are, whether or not they are real. Metaphysics, if it can say what is real, seems relevant only to the first interpretation. But a thing's being real is not a reason for thinking it good. Further, the view that we need to know reality, to know what is supremely good, loses credibility, once we see that no practical rule of conduct can be true, if the sole reality is eternal, or it is the sole good. **71** For ethical purposes, metaphysical construction of reality would be as helpful if it were of an imaginary utopia, as this would still provide material for value judgements. Metaphysics may suggest possible ideals, of which we would not otherwise have thought, and which we may see to be good, but their being real would not make them more useful. **72** Metaphysicians see metaphysics as the sole basis of ethics, because they think that proving something supersensibly real also proves it is good. They believe that good means having some supersensible property, so ethical questions can be answered by identifying things that have it. **73** They see that 'good' is a predicate that neither does nor can exist, but conclude it means being related to something which exists in supersensible reality, and so commit the naturalistic fallacy with regard to its meaning.

74 Misconceptions also arise from calling what ought to be done a 'moral law'. **75** Kant's mistake is to make moral law analogous to natural law, by identifying what ought to be with the law by which a free or pure will must act, so that there is no separate standard for judging it. As this moral law depends on freedom, no claim about a thing's being good can be true, unless reality is as he says, and the will is free. **76** Another of his fallacies is to regard the moral law as an imperative, making 'what ought to be' mean 'what is commanded', ultimately by a real supersensible authority: but what is commanded is only a source of moral obligation, if it is good.

77 A common assumption of contemporary metaphysical ethics is that ethical questions can be answered by investigating the nature of the will, linking up with the view that a thing's reality or truth relates to its being known in a certain way: that metaphysical propositions relate to cognition, ethical ones to the will. **78** Since Kant, cognition and volition have been seen as distinct attitudes of mind towards reality. **79** This could mean that we become aware of ethical distinctions through willing (a purely psychological fact), or that our willing a thing is the same as thinking it good. **80** But preferring a thing does not show it is good, only that we think it so, while it is false to think that a thing's being true is the same as its being thought in a certain way. **81** To say a thing is perceived is not only to say the mind is cognitive, but also that what it cognizes is true and, if the thing supposedly perceived is untrue, it is not perceived. **82** Just as the question of what is true is confused with that of what is thought true, so is that of what is good with that of what is thought good. It is held that the difference between them concerns a difference of volition. **83** The most that it might be possible to say is that what is willed in a certain way is always also good, which would make its being thus willed a criterion of its goodness. **84** Philosophers who base their ethics on investigation of will think goodness is identical with being willed, and so commit the naturalistic fallacy.

85 This section summarizes the contents of the chapter.

Chapter V *Ethics in Relation to Conduct (pp. 192–231)*

86 All ethical propositions are based, ultimately, on a proposition that cannot be logically deduced from any other; the fundamental principles of ethics are self-evident. **87** It was not possible to prove the untruth of the proposition that it is self-evident that pleasure is the only good, but it does contradict other apparently true propositions. **88** Chapter V concerns decisions about what is right, or what we ought to do, which involve both ethical judgements and empirical investigation of the kind of effects particular actions produce. **89** All such questions are about the cause of a good effect, and, when ethics prescribes duties, it means acting in ways (as in the duty not to commit murder) that will always produce the greatest possible sum of good.

90 Intuitionists, who say that what is right is, like what is good in itself, intuitively certain, are wrong, as investigation of causes and effects can confirm the former. **91** But ethics cannot give a definite list of duties, as this would require information about all the future effects of a possible action and their value. The best to be hoped for is to show which possible action is likely to produce the most good. **92** This will suffice for practical guidance. **93** Even establishing the probability that a particular action will produce a better total result than another is very difficult. No sufficient reason has ever been given for thinking one action more right or wrong than another, as the effects of different possible actions can only be calculated over a short period. **94** No ethical law can be more than a generalization; all practical ethics can do is lay down general rules about which of a few alternative actions will generally produce the greatest balance of good in the short term. **95** Most of the rules, endorsed by common-sense morality, are of this type, such as those prohibiting murder; and such rules are essential to the preservation of civilized society. **96** But the usefulness of some rules of common-sense morality seems to depend on temporary social conditions. **97** Legal penalties and social disapproval are also reasons for obeying such rules, and for regarding the actions they prohibit as generally wrong.

98 A lot of effort is spent on encouraging people to obey rules that are not generally practised, when it is doubtful that ethics can ever show the usefulness of any rules, apart from generally practised ones. **99** A generally useful and practised rule should always be observed. It may not always be useful, but people are unlikely to be able to decide correctly when it will not be, and they will set a bad example to others, if they do not follow it. **100** When there is no generally practised rule to hand, people should consider the intrinsic value or badness of possible actions' effects, and act accordingly. An achievable lesser good, attainable in the near future, is preferable to a less achievable, or remote, greater one. **101** A duty is simply a means to good. The only important distinction in ethics is between what is good in itself and what is good as a means. Duties are actions that attract moral approval, and which people are tempted to omit: not doing them generally harms others. Expedient actions are ones people are inclined to perform, as they benefit the agent, but this does not mean the former are more useful than latter. **102** Interested actions are those where the effects on the agent are the best possible, which will not necessarily produce the best possible results on the whole. The main difference between duty and interest is that the latter action has its main effects on the agent, and so he is not inclined to omit it.

103 Aristotle says virtue is a habitual disposition to act in certain ways, and virtues are usually regarded as having intrinsic value. But the same test, of whether it is a means to good, should be applied to a virtue as to a duty. Virtue can be defined as a habitual disposition to carry out actions that usually produce the best possible results, which are generally duties. **104** Only intuition can decide if virtues and duties are good in themselves. Intrinsic value is a simple and unique notion, and what ought to be done, because it has intrinsic value, must be distinguished from what ought to be done as a means to it. Virtue is a means to good, and is no more the sole good than pleasure, but, as virtues are complex, they are more likely to include things that are good in themselves. **105** Most virtues have no intrinsic value, and are not the sole good. Kant says virtue makes people worthy of happiness, contradicting his claim that only a good will has intrinsic value, by suggesting that a state combining virtue and happiness is better in itself than one without the latter.

106 People perform duties, without thinking whether any good will result from them. It is useful for a virtue to be habitual, but absurd to describe a disposition to perform an action, which has only external rightness, as good in itself. **107** When performing a duty, a person may feel a love of some intrinsically good consequence, which he expects his action to produce; and Christianity is right to stress the importance of inward disposition. But the New Testament's concern with promoting such virtues as justice and mercy, which are good as means, must be distinguished from its insistence that being angry without cause is as bad as actually committing murder. Jesus may be right that an angry man's state is as bad as a murderer's, but the implication that it causes as much evil is wrong. Christianity praises things that are good as means, as if they were good in themselves, and vice versa. **108** Christianity stresses the value of the feeling excited by the idea of an action's rightness. This idea of abstract rightness constitutes the conscience. The emotion, excited by rightness, is intrinsically valuable, but not more so than love of things good in themselves. Though generally useful, harmful actions may result from conscientious motives, which are not an infallible guide to right actions.

109 This section summarizes the contents of the chapter.

Chapter VI   The Ideal (pp. 232–73)

110 This may be the best state of things conceivable (absolute good), the best we could possibly bring about (utopia), or what is good in itself in a high degree. Chapter VI addresses the third sense. **111** This relates to the other two because, although the absolute good may consist of things that cannot be imagined, there is no reason to think that what cannot be imagined is better than things that can. The search for the ideal will be confined to one for a whole, which, though not certainly perfection, seems better than the rest, and will consist of as many things with positive value as possible, with nothing evil or indifferent in it. One problem with many accounts of the ideal has been omitting many things of positive value, by limiting them to the best of single things. But there are many positive goods, and any whole containing them all must be very complex. Utopias, by contrast, are often thought of as consisting of mere means to good, indifferent things, and exclusion of great positive evils. But, deciding what ought to be aimed at requires consideration, not only of what is obtainable, but of what has the greatest value, so comparative valuation of known goods is as relevant to investigation of utopias as to the absolute good.

112 Determining what has intrinsic value requires identifying the things that would be judged good, if they existed by themselves, and then determining their comparative value. **113** The most valuable things are the pleasures of human relationships and enjoyment of beautiful objects. Moral philosophy's fundamental truth is that it is only for their sake that there is any purpose in doing any public or private duty, or being virtuous. These complex wholes are the rational ultimate end of human action. **114** Appreciation of a beautiful object includes both bare cognition of what is beautiful and an appropriate emotion. But, as the wholes are organic, the emotion alone would not necessarily have value, and might be bad, if applied to something ugly. **115** The emotion and the cognitive element, which also has little value by itself, must both be present to form these highly valuable wholes. The former is the actual consciousness of the object's beautiful qualities.

116 Seeing beauty in something that has it is better than seeing it in something that does not, but the latter could mean, either ascribing to an object really beautiful qualities it lacks, or having for actual qualities that are not beautiful a feeling, only appropriate if they were. The first is an error of judgement, involving a false judgment of fact; the second, one of taste, involving a false judgement of value. The second has no value, apart from the emotion: seeing beauty in a thing lacking it is less valuable than seeing it where it actually is. With the first, there is cognition of really beautiful qualities, and an appropriate emotion, but what is believed about the object is false. So, where there is cognition of beautiful qualities and the appropriate emotion, there may also be: belief in the existence of these qualities, and they exist; mere cognition, without belief, when it is either true, or false, that they exist; belief in the existence of the qualities, and they do not exist. The first relates to appreciation of natural beauty and human affections; the second defines the pleasures of imagination, including appreciation of works of art; the third relates to misdirected affection, and may include a believer's love of God.

117 With imaginative appreciations, where there is no belief in the cognized object's existence or non-existence, the issue of existence has no effect on the total state's value. With the other two, belief in the object's reality makes the state better, if true, worse, if not. This vindicates the view that knowledge, as opposed to belief in what is false, or mere awareness of what is true, can make a whole more valuable: those with a high regard for truth tend to believe a poet's contemplation of the kingdom of heaven is superior to the religious believer's, if it does not exist.

118 With belief, its object's truth or falsity affects its value as a means: we are likely to act on our beliefs, so their being true rules out disappointment. Belief in God may make the believer do things that, if he does not exist, are worse than the things he might have done otherwise. 119 The object's existence as a whole also seems to add to its value. If someone's life consisted of contemplating beautiful scenery, and interacting with admirable people, but they were unreal, such a world would be regarded as greatly inferior in value to one in which

they existed, both for that reason and because this person's belief would be false.

120 Aesthetic and affectionate enjoyments lack value without cognition of appropriate objects; this lacks value without the appropriate emotion; and thus a whole, combining both, has much greater value than the sum of the values of its parts. If belief in the object's reality is added, the new whole's value greatly exceeds the sum obtained by the addition of the value of the true belief, considered by itself, to that of the original wholes. This seems to vindicate the great intrinsic value attached to mere knowledge of some truths. Even where there is great inferiority in the value of an emotion and the beauty of its object, combining true belief with them may create a whole equal or superior in value to those where the former is superior, but the latter is lacking. God may be more perfect than any human being, but love of God may be inferior to human love, if he does not exist.

121 The naturalistic fallacy occurs in relation to beauty, as it is claimed that 'beautiful' can be defined as what has certain effects upon our feelings, whereas a thing's beauty is determined by the objective issue of whether or not it is truly good, explaining the connection between goodness and beauty. Although 'good' is the only unanalysable predicate of value, 'beautiful' is defined by reference to it: proving something beautiful means that the whole, of which it is part, is truly good. There is no single criterion of beauty; the specific qualities that make one beautiful object different from others are as essential to its beauty as any generic qualities it shares with them.

122 With personal affection, the object is of great intrinsic value, and must be both truly beautiful and good. Much of the most valuable affection concerns mental qualities, but appreciation of appropriate physical qualities makes it more so. The most valuable appreciation of a person seems to be of their attitude towards others. Love of love is a far more valuable good than mere love of beauty, but only seems to be so, if it includes the latter. As to the nature of the mental qualities that have to be cognized, to make human relationships valuable, they include the various emotions appropriate to persons, as well as to mere corporeal beauty.

123 Many philosophers, who accept pleasure is not the sole good, and that it is complex, regard it as a purely spiritual state. But valuable things are organic unities that include cognition of material qualities as apparently essential elements: a purely spiritual good may be the best single thing, but adding appreciation of material qualities seems to give a greater sum of value. **124** Great positive evils are organic unities: cognitions of an object, together with an emotion. Neither, by itself, seems capable of being greatly evil, but a whole, formed of both, does. There are three classes. **125** The first is admiring contemplation of what is evil. Lust and cruelty, for example, are bad as means and in themselves. Both involve love of evil: the first, enjoyment of the same state of mind in others, the second, pleasure in others' pain. Cruelty is equally odious, whether the pain is real or imaginary, so true belief in their objects' existence has no relevance to evils of this sort. **126** Mixed evils involve cognition of what is good, together with an inappropriate emotion: hating the good. They are made worse by true belief in the existence of the hated good object. **127** The third class, pain, would not be an evil without consciousness of it. The difference between it and pleasure is that, while the latter is not a great good by itself, the former is a great evil by itself. **128** Neither pleasure, nor pain, necessarily makes a state of things respectively better or worse, on the whole, than they would otherwise be. **129** Mixed goods are positively good as wholes, but include intrinsically evil elements.

130 A whole, such as retributive punishment, comprising two positive evils, wickedness and pain, may not be positively good, on the whole, but may be a lesser evil than either of its parts. Thus, if an evil already exists, it may be worth creating another, as this may produce a less bad whole, than if the original evil had been allowed to exist alone.

131 Mixed goods are such virtues as courage and compassion, which require cognition of something evil and hatred of it. Pity for others' suffering seems admirable in itself, and would not exist without cognition of evil. The moral sentiment, relating to the ideas of right and wrong, involves cognizing something intrinsically evil, and having an emotion of hatred for it.

132 With many virtues, the value of a great good depends on the presence of something evil. Conscious compassion for actual suffering seems better, as a whole, despite the fact that the evil of actual suffering makes the total situation bad on the whole.

133 While the appropriate mental attitude towards a real evil is a positive good, the former will always bring the total value down to a negative amount, ruling out the paradox that, in an ideal world, actual suffering must exist, so compassion can be felt; imaginary ones would suffice. Thus, the arguments in theodicies must be rejected: there is no justification for even the smallest of the world's evils. A whole lacking such virtues as compassion would not be as good, on the whole, as one containing them. Where evils already exist, as in the world, it has greater value, as a whole, for them to be pitied or hated, as actual evils, not imaginary ones, although this is never positively good, on the whole. **134** Many and various things are intrinsically good or bad, and most are organic unities. The only way to decide their intrinsic value is to identify them clearly, and see if they have the unique predicate, 'good'.

135 This section summarizes the contents of the chapter.

Glossary

Absolute good. See *summum bonum* below.

Absolute idealism. System of philosophy, deriving from that of Hegel, which maintains that, contrary to the empiricist view of the world (that it consists of many different things, which we know through our senses), ultimate reality is unified and whole, and is to be identified with the one absolute mind or spirit.

Abstract rightness. See internal rightness below.

Acts necessary for preservation of life. Those things which people have to do, in order to remain alive. In Chapter II, Moore rejects the view that only these should be regarded as good.

Aesthetic enjoyments. Enjoyment that involves appreciation of beautiful objects.

Agent. One who performs an action.

Ambiguous form of ethical questions. Ethical questions are sometimes expressed in a way that is capable of more than one interpretation.

Analogy. Drawing a parallel between two things on the basis of similarities between them.

Analysis/analytic approach to philosophy. Breaking complex objects of thought down, until the process can go no further, and their simple parts (Moore calls them 'ultimate terms of reference') are reached. This was Moore's approach to philosophy.

Analytic (proposition). One in which the predicate is included in the subject, or where denying it would be self-contradictory, as in 'This house is a building.' They are *a priori* propositions, that is, they come before experience, and hold irrespective of experience. Moore argues that propositions about 'good' are never analytic, because it is not possible to decide what 'good' means simply through analysis of the term itself. See also synthetic below

Appeal to nature. Trying to base ethical values on nature; holding that what is natural must be good. See Chapter II.

Glossary

Aristotle (384–322 BC). Greek philosopher, student of Plato and author of such books as *Nicomachean Ethics, De Interpretatione* and the *Metaphysics*. Aristotle's analysis of virtues is discussed in Chapter V.

Axiom. Principle or maxim.

Balance of good. That the consequences of an action, over time, will produce more good than evil, on the whole.

Bentham, Jeremy (1748–1832). Founder of utilitarianism, friend of John Stuart Mill and his father, the philosopher, James Mill, and author of *A Fragment on Government* and an *Introduction to the Principles of Morals and Legislation*. Bentham's ethical theories are referred to in Chapter I.

Bloomsbury Group. The name (deriving from the part of London where Virginia Woolf and her husband lived) given to the group of writers, artists and intellectuals (it also included Lytton Strachey and John Maynard Keynes) who were influenced by Moore's *Principia Ethica* and its emphasis on appreciation of beauty and friendship.

Bradley, Francis Herbert (1846–1924). Oxford philosopher, advocate of absolute idealism and author of *Appearance and Reality, Ethical Studies* and *Principles of Logic*.

Brentano, Franz (1838–1917). German philosopher, psychologist, theologian and author of *Origin of the Knowledge of Right and Wrong*.

Casuistry. Working out detailed ethical rules to cover specific situations and circumstances.

Causal truths. Accurate information about the results caused by a particular action.

Charity. Loving attitude towards other human beings, giving of money/relief to the poor.

Chastity. Not engaging in unlawful sexual relationships.

Cognition/cognize. (Faculty of) knowing or perceiving.

Common or peculiar properties. That things that are good or evil in themselves may not have any qualities they share, or which are distinctive of them, other than being good or evil.

Common-sense morality. Generally accepted moral rules, which common sense suggests people should follow.

Commonest rules of conduct. The most generally accepted and followed rules of conduct.

Complex. Having many parts.

Conjugal. Relating to marriage.

Conscience. Human beings' awareness of what is right or wrong, which deters them from acting in certain ways. Moore (Chapter V) relates it to a sense of an action's internal rightness.

Consciousness. State of being aware, of knowing.

Consequentialist (moral system). Moral system which decides whether an action is right or wrong on the basis of its consequences. See also utilitarianism below.

Corporeal. Bodily.

Criterion of ethical value. Standard for deciding what is good or bad, right or wrong.

Darwin, Charles Robert (1809–92). Scientist, naturalist and author of *The Origin of Species by Means of Natural Selection*, who developed the theory of evolution.

Deontological intuitionist. Moral philosopher/moralist, who holds that what is right, as well as what is good in itself, can be known through intuition. See also intuition(s) below.

Divine omnipotence. Monotheistic religions, such as Christianity, teach that God's power is unlimited, so he is all-powerful or omnipotent.

Doctrine. What is taught, belief or tenet.

Duty. That which the law, or a set of moral principles, requires/obliges us to do. Moore defines duty as that which is a 'means to good', or the 'best possible'.

Egoism. Moral system based on self-interest. Different forms of egoism are discussed in Chapter III.

Empiricism/empirical/empiricist. What relates to, is based on, experience. Empiricists maintain that (sense) experience is the (principal) source of knowledge.

End. That which is desired or aimed at.

Eternal (reality). Here, without beginning or end, that which transcends time.

Ethics/ethical. Terms generally used interchangeably with morality/moral; set of moral principles that tell us what is good or bad, right or wrong, the (philosophical) study of what is good and right.

Ethical non-naturalist. Moral philosopher/moralist, who believes that goodnesss is a non-natural property that a particular thing, or state of affairs, has.

Ethical philosopher. See moral philosophy below.

Ethical principle. Moral truth or rule.

Ethical truths of our first or self-evident class. Things which are good in themselves, which possess the simple, unanalysable and non-natural quality of being good, and which are known by intuition.

Evil. That which is harmful and opposed to good.

Glossary

Evolution. The gradual development of, and changes in, plant and animal life, in response to their environment. See Darwin above.

Evolutionist. See evolutionist ethics below.

Evolutionist ethics. The view that morality should, in some way, be based on, or reflect, evolution, as it shows what we ought to do, and how we ought to develop. These theories are discussed in Chapter II.

Exercise the judgment of value. Make a value judgement about, try to determine whether something is good or bad.

Exist for their own sakes. Things that are good in themselves.

Exist in time. Moore defines a natural object as something that exists in time.

Expedient. That which is considered useful or convenient for accomplishing a specific purpose.

Experience. What relates to the empirical world and the way human beings experience things.

External rightness. Where the right thing is done from habit (Moore gives the example of not stealing) without any thought as to whether it will do any good.

Fallacy. Erroneous belief or opinion.

False antithesis. Where words or ideas appear to be the direct opposites of each other, but are not.

First principle(s) (of morality). The basic principle(s) of a moral system, which are incapable of direct proof.

Free or pure will. Kant (*Groundwork of the Metaphysics of Morals*) regards freedom of the will as the supreme principle of morality. Although subject to laws of nature, human beings, as rational beings, are free, and able to subject themselves to moral laws discovered by their reason. Freedom cannot be proved, but must be presupposed, in order for there to be moral responsibility.

Fundamental moral principle. See first principle above.

Fundamental principles of ethical reasoning. The basic rules of how to reason about ethical questions.

General happiness. Utilitarianism is not concerned only with promoting the agent's own happiness, but with promoting general happiness. See also greatest happiness below.

General law. General moral principle or rule.

General rules. General moral rules, general rules to guide conduct.

Generic qualities. Qualities that are characteristic or typical of a particular class of things.

God. Moore does not discuss God in the context of any particular religion, but the attributes (for example, omnipotence) and con-

Glossary

cepts (kingdom of heaven) relate to Christianity.

Good and evil in themselves. Those things which are intrinsically or essentially good or evil.

Good as a means. That which leads to, or produces, something that is good in itself.

Good will. A will that carries out moral duties for their own sake, and not for personal advantage, to satisfy desires, or because of their consequences. In the *Groundwork of the Metaphysics of Morals*, Kant says that it is the only thing that is good without qualification.

Greater sum of intrinsic value. A greater quantity of things that are good in themselves.

Greatest happiness. The (utilitarian) idea that right actions are those which maximize the happiness of the greatest number of people.

Green, Thomas Hill (1836–82). Oxford philosopher and author of the *Prolegomena to Ethics*.

Heaven. Traditionally, the place where God dwells, and to which Christians hope to go, if they lead virtuous lives.

Hedonism. The philosophical view that pleasure is the main or only thing that is good.

Hedonistic principle. See hedonism above.

Hegel, Georg Wilhelm Friedrich (1770–1831). German philosopher, professor of philosophy at Berlin, and author of such works as *The Phenomenology of Mind* and *The Philosophy of Right*.

Hobbes, Thomas (1588–1679). British philosopher and author of the *Elements of Law, Human Nature* and *Leviathan*.

Hypothesis. A theory put forward as a basis for reasoning, or a starting-point for discussion.

Identical proposition. Proposition that appears to refer to two notions but, in fact, only refers to one.

Imperative. Command, sentence expressing a command. According to Kant (*Groundwork of the Metaphysics of Morals*), moral principles are categorical imperatives: they command unconditionally.

Indifferent. Here, things that are neither good nor bad.

Inductive reasoning. The most common form of reasoning, which infers probable conclusions from premises based on experience.

Inference/infer. Concluding one thing from something else.

Internal rightness. That a particular course of action is intrinsically right/right in itself, not just a means to good.

Intrinsic value. (That which is) good in itself, essentially good.

Intrinsic worth. See intrinsic value above.

Intrinsically good. That which is good in itself.

Glossary

Intuitionistic Hedonism. That it can be known, by intuition, that pleasure alone is good as an end.

Intuition(s). Immediate mental awareness/apprehension. Moore holds that the truth of propositions about things being good or evil in themselves can only be known through intuition: the truth of such propositions cannot be proved or disproved.

Inward disposition. The (positive) attitude towards, feeling about, an action and its (good) consequence(s).

Ipso facto. By that very fact.

Jesus (Christ) (c. 5/6 BC–c. AD 30). Founder of Christianity. Some of Jesus' ethical teachings are referred to in Chapter V.

Kant, Immanuel (1724–1804). German philosopher, professor of philosophy at Königsberg and author of such works as *Critique of Pure Reason*, *Critique of Practical Reason* and *Groundwork of the Metaphysics of Morals*. Kant's ethical theories are referred to in Chapter IV.

Keynes, John Maynard, Baron Keynes of Tilton (1883–1946). Cambridge economist, whose economic theories were a major influence on the development of post-Second World War economic policies, and who advocated establishment of the International Monetary Fund. His books include *General Theory of Employment, Interest and Money*, and *Treatise on Money*.

Kingdom of Ends. Kant's idea (*Groundwork of the Metaphysics of Morals*) of a 'moral kingdom', which human beings, as rational beings, can create, by always treating themselves and others as ends in themselves, not means. Human beings should always behave as if they are members of such a kingdom.

Kingdom of Heaven. Here, just heaven (see above), but also used as an alternative term for the coming kingdom of God that Jesus preached about.

Lasciviousness. Lustfulness, lewdness.

Law(s) of nature. Generalization(s), based on experience and scientific observation, about the (predictable) ways in which the universe operates.

Lexicographical question. Question about the use or meaning of a word, its dictionary definition.

Logical. Science of inference or reasoning.

Maxim of prudence. A rule of conduct that is sensible or worldly-wise: in particular, the individual making pursuit of his own happiness his principal end.

McTaggart, John McTaggart Ellis (1866–1925). Cambridge idealist philosopher and author of *The Nature of Existence*.

Metaethics. See Moral philosophy below.

Metaphysical/metaphysical ethics. Ethical theories that define 'good' in relation to an object that does not exist in the ordinary physical world, but in what Moore calls a 'supersensible real world' (see below).

Metaphysician. Here, philosopher who believes in the existence of a supersensible reality, and its relevance to ethics.

Metaphysics. Study of what is after (beyond) physics, and which cannot be investigated by ordinary empirical methods; the investigation of what really exists, of ultimate reality.

Mill, John Stuart (1806–73). Utilitarian philosopher and author of *Utilitarianism, On Liberty* and *The Subjection of Women*. Mill's ethical theories are discussed in Chapter III.

Mixed evils. Cognizing what is good, but having an inappropriate emotion towards it, such as hating what is good or beautiful.

Mixed goods. Good wholes that contain evil or ugly elements.

Modern philosophy. Here, philosophy after Hegel, philosophy during the nineteenth century.

Moral exhortation. Urging others to adopt, and practise, a particular moral principle(s).

Moral law. The *a priori* moral principles, discovered by reason, which should govern the actions of rational beings (Kant, *Groundwork of the Metaphysics of Morals*).

Moral philosopher. See moral philosophy below.

Moral philosophy. Branch of philosophy concerned with moral issues and the general principles of morality. It can be concerned with trying to decide what is right and wrong and why we should adopt/follow a certain set of moral principles, or, more narrowly (metaethics), with the nature of moral argument and the meaning and use of such moral terms as 'good' and 'right'.

More extended beneficence. Doing good on a wide(r) scale.

Mutual causal dependence. Things, like the parts of the body, that are interdependent.

Mutually means and ends to one another. Things, like the parts of the body, that are causes and effects of each other.

Natural law(s). See law(s) of nature above.

Natural object. An object of experience, one that exists in time.

Natural sciences. Sciences which use empirical methods to explore the physical world.

Natural selection. Darwin's theory that the animal species that have

Glossary

been able to adapt to their environment are the ones that have survived: the survival of the fittest.

Naturalism. See naturalistic ethics and naturalistic fallacy below.

Naturalistic ethics. Ethical theories that define 'good' by reference to a natural object, which is an object of experience. Moore discusses these in Chapters II and III.

Naturalistic fallacy. The name Moore gives to the fallacy of confusing good with/defining it as a natural property or object, such as pleasure (see Chapter I). He accuses a number of philosophers, including Mill, of committing this fallacy.

Naturalistic hedonism. Defining good as that which produces pleasure/happiness.

Necessary condition. That which has to be present, in order for something else to exist.

New Testament. The part of the Bible concerned with the life and teaching of Jesus and the early history of Christianity. Aspects of the ethical teaching found in the New Testament, are referred to in Chapter V.

Newton, Isaac (1642–1727). English physicist and mathematician, who put forward the law of universal gravitation in his *Philosophiae Naturalis Principia Mathematica*.

Notion. Idea, conception.

Object of intuition. That which can be known by intuition.

Obligatory. That which we are required to do (by the particular moral system to which we subscribe).

Open question. Whatever is said to be good, it is always an open question (the question can be asked intelligibly) whether it is good, so nothing can be good by definition. For example, many people may believe that pleasure/happiness is the only good, but the question whether it is makes sense. See Chapters I and II.

Organic whole/unity/relation. This refers to the relationship between a whole and its constituent parts, where the whole has an intrinsic value different from the sum of the values of its parts.

Paradox. Statement/something that appears, but may not be, absurd or self-contradictory.

Partially identical. Partly the same as.

Personal affections. Loving personal relationships.

Philosopher. One who studies and practises/teaches philosophy.

Philosophy. Literally, love of wisdom. The study of ultimate reality, what really exists, the most general principles of things.

Plato (c. 429–347 BC). Greek philosopher and pupil of Socrates, who founded the Academy (the world's first university) in Athens, where Aristotle studied, and whose many writings include *The Republic, Theaetetus, Symposium, Phaedrus* and *Laws*.

Pleasure alone is good. See hedonism above.

Practical ethics. Branch of ethics concerned with what human beings ought to do.

Practical maxim. Rule of conduct that is actually followed.

Practical principles. Moral principles, rules of conduct that are actually followed

Prayer Book. The Anglican Book of Common Prayer.

Predicate. The part of a statement/proposition in which something is said about the subject.

Premise. One of the propositions in an argument, on the basis of which the conclusion is reached.

Principle of organic unities/principle of organic relations. The principle that a whole may have an intrinsic value different from the sum of the values of its parts. See Organic whole/unity/relation above and Chapter III.

Principle of rational benevolence. See utilitarian duty below.

Probability. What is most likely to happen.

Property. Attribute or quality.

Proposition. Statement, which may or may not be true.

Protarchus. Socrates' interlocutor in Plato's *Philebus*.

Psychology. Scientific study of the human mind.

Psychological Hedonism. The ethical view that pleasure alone is good, because it is really the only thing that is desired.

Quality of pleasure. The worth or value of a pleasure. In *Utilitarianism*, Mill distinguishes between higher and lower pleasures, and argues that the quality of a pleasure is more important than its quantity.

Quantity of pleasure. The amount of pleasure, as opposed to the quality of a pleasure.

Questions of ultimate ends. Questions as to what is ultimately desirable or valuable.

Representative art. Paintings, works of art that portray scenes from life.

Retributive punishment. Punishment designed to exact revenge, or pay the offender back for what he has done.

Right action. See duty above.

Rousseau, Jean-Jacques (1712–78). Swiss philosopher and author of *Émile, or Education* and *The Social Contract*. His ethical theories are referred to in Chapter II.

Russell, Bertrand Arthur William, Third Earl Russell (1872–1970).

Glossary

British philosopher, mathematician, writer and peace campaigner, and grandson of Whig prime minister, Lord John Russell (First Earl Russell). Fellow of Trinity College, Cambridge, and author of *Principia Mathematica, The Problems of Philosophy, History of Western Philosophy* and *Why I am not a Christian*.

Sanctions. Penalties designed to secure performance of a duty, or obedience to a rule.

Scientific Ethics. The kind of thorough and systematic study of ethical theory that Moore undertakes in *Principia Ethica*.

Self-contradictory. When what is asserted negates itself.

Sensual indulgence. (Extensive) enjoyment of physical pleasures, such as sex and food.

Sidgwick, Henry (1838–1900). Cambridge philosopher, campaigner for the rights and education of women and author of the *Methods of Ethics*. Sidgwick's ethical theories are discussed in Chapter III.

Simplest terms. Most basic component parts.

Sociology. Academic discipline concerned with the study of society.

Socrates (c. 470–399 BC). Athenian philosopher, who devoted his life to pursuit of philosophical truth, but who was executed for undermining belief in the gods and corrupting youth.

Spencer, Herbert (1820–1903). Journalist, philosopher and writer about science, whose works include *The Principles of Psychology* and *Education*. Spencer's ethical theories are discussed in Chapter II.

Strachey, Giles Lytton (1880–1932). Intellectual, biographer and literary critic of the *Spectator*, whose books include *Eminent Victorians, Queen Victoria* and *Elizabeth and Essex*.

Substantive. Old term for a noun.

Summum bonum. The highest or maximum good, what is good without qualification.

Supersensible real world/supersensible reality. A world/reality that is beyond/ transcends the ordinary physical world that we know about through experience/the senses.

Survival of the fittest. See natural selection above.

Synthetic (proposition). One which gives actual information. Generally, it is held that synthetic propositions are also *a posteriori*, that is, they derive the information they give from experience. See also analytic above.

Synthetic activity. The synthesizing activity of the mind, by which it builds concepts/propositions into a unified whole.

Tautology. Saying something twice in different ways.

The value of the whole must not be assumed to be the same as the sum

of the values of its parts. See principle of organic unities/principle of organic relations above.

Theodicy(ies). Arguments that attempt to reconcile belief in an infinitely powerful and benevolent God, who made the world, with the fact that the world contains evil and suffering.

Theory of natural selection. See natural selection above.

Universal ethical judgment. An ethical judgement that is always true, that relates to everybody and applies in all situations.

Universal ethical principle. Fundamental ethical truth or rule.

Universal good. The only thing that is good.

Universal sanction. General approval or confirmation.

Universalistic hedonism. The ethical view that general happiness is the sole good.

Universally true causal judgments. Unfailingly accurate judgements about the effects actions will produce.

Utilitarian duty. The duty to promote general happiness.

Utilitarianism/utilitarians. A consequentialist moral system (one which decides whether an action is right or wrong on the basis of its consequences), which holds that actions are not right or wrong in themselves, but only to the extent to which they promote pleasure/happiness and prevent pain. Moore discusses, and rejects, utilitarian theories in Chapter III.

Utility. Usefulness.

Utopia. Way of referring to a place or state of affairs that is perfect or ideal, deriving from a book of that title by Sir Thomas More.

Valid reasons. Reasons that are logically sound, well-grounded.

Verbal discussion. Discussion about the use or meaning of words.

Virtue. Goodness, moral excellence, admirable quality of character. Individual virtues include charity, patience and humility.

Volition. Act of willing.

Whatever definition of good is given, it may always be asked, with significance, of the complex so defined, whether it is itself good. See open question argument above.

Will. The capability of wishing for something and using one's mental powers to try to accomplish it. See Chapter IV.

Wittgenstein, Ludwig Josef Johan (1889–1951). Austrian-born exponent of analytical philosophy, who studied philosophy at Cambridge, where he became professor of philosophy. Author of *Tractatus Logico-Philosophicus* and (posthumously) *Philosophical Investigations*.

Woolf, Virginia (1882–1941). Novelist and literary critic, whose books include *Mrs Dalloway*, *To the Lighthouse* and *The Waves*.